COVID-19 and Public Policy in the Digital Age

COVID-19 and Public Policy in the Digital Age explores how states and societies have responded to the COVID-19 pandemic and their long-term implications for public policy and the rule of law globally. It examines the extent to which existing methods of protecting public safety and national security measure up in a time of crisis. The volume also examines how these ideas themselves have undergone transformation in the context of the global crisis.

This book:

- Explores the intersection of public policy, individual rights, and technology;
- Analyzes the role of science in determining political choices;
- Reconsiders our understanding of security studies on a global scale arising out of antisocial behaviour, panic buying, and stockpiling of food and (in the United States) arms;
- Probes the role of fake news and social media in crisis situations; and
- Provides a critical analysis of the notion of global surveillance in relation to the pandemic.

A timely, prescient volume on the many ramifications of the pandemic, this book will be essential reading for professionals, scholars, researchers, and students of public policy, especially practitioners working in the fields of technology and society, security studies, law, media studies, and public health.

Andrea Monti is an Italian lawyer, journalist, and academic, whose expertise ranges from biotechnology to privacy and high-tech law. He is Adjunct Professor of Public Order and Security at the Gabriele d'Annunzio University of Chieti, Italy. Over the last two years, he delivered lectures as part of the Italian State Police training programmes. He has published several papers on bio-information, computer forensics, technology, and public order, as well as books on computer hacking. His most recent publication is *Protecting Personal Information: The Right to Privacy Reconsidered*, with Raymond Wacks (2019).

Raymond Wacks is Emeritus Professor of Law and Legal Theory at the University of Hong Kong. He has published more than twenty books which have been translated into a dozen languages. His works include *Personal Information: Privacy and the Law*; *Privacy and Media Freedom*; *Privacy: A Very Short Introduction*; and *Law: A Very Short Introduction*. His most recent publication is *Protecting Personal Information: The Right to Privacy Reconsidered*, with Andrea Monti (2019). The sixth edition of his *Understanding Jurisprudence: An Introduction to Legal Theory* was published in 2020.

COVID-19 and Public Policy in the Digital Age

Andrea Monti and Raymond Wacks

LONDON AND NEW YORK

First published 2021
by Routledge
2 Park Square, Milton Park, Abingdon, Oxon OX14 4RN

and by Routledge
52 Vanderbilt Avenue, New York, NY 10017

Routledge is an imprint of the Taylor & Francis Group, an informa business

© 2021 Andrea Monti and Raymond Wacks

The right of Andrea Monti and Raymond Wacks to be identified as authors of this work has been asserted by them in accordance with sections 77 and 78 of the Copyright, Designs and Patents Act 1988.

All rights reserved. No part of this book may be reprinted or reproduced or utilised in any form or by any electronic, mechanical, or other means, now known or hereafter invented, including photocopying and recording, or in any information storage or retrieval system, without permission in writing from the publishers.

Trademark notice: Product or corporate names may be trademarks or registered trademarks, and are used only for identification and explanation without intent to infringe.

British Library Cataloguing-in-Publication Data
A catalogue record for this book is available from the British Library

Library of Congress Cataloging-in-Publication Data
A catalog record has been requested for this book

ISBN: 978-0-367-55345-6 (hbk)
ISBN: 978-0-367-56023-2 (pbk)
ISBN: 978-1-003-09612-2 (ebk)

Typeset in Sabon
by Deanta Global Publishing Services, Chennai, India

Contents

	Preface	vi
	Acknowledgements	viii
1	Confronting contagion	1
2	Science and power	15
3	Law, rights, and public policy	48
4	The technology of information	81
5	The politics of the pandemic	112
	Epilogue	139
	Index	142

Preface

Plagues, as Camus reminds us, recur, yet we find it difficult to believe that they 'crash down on our heads from a blue sky'. The effects of the precipitous transformation of the world will linger not only in the deaths, suffering, and economic devastation wrought by the novel Coronavirus, but in our reluctant acknowledgement that we are vulnerable. The advances in medicine, science, and technology may mitigate, but cannot always prevent the malevolence of disease.

This book began as an analysis of the complexities of, and relationship between, national security, public policy, and digital technologies. In the course of writing, however, the pandemic intervened and we found ourselves increasingly driven toward its numerous consequences. Is it 'simply' a medical emergency? Or is it primarily a national security problem? The crackdown on the digital exercise of fundamental rights is—or could be—justified in the name of security? Can we trust Big Tech to play a critical role in managing the containment of the contagion? We eventually concluded that the focus of the book ought to be on the disquieting implications of the latter question, uncertain where it would take us.

It raised an associated matter: the effects of COVID-19 on the rule of law and fundamental rights. We therefore analyzed the extent to which cultural differences shaped public policy to the pandemic. We investigated the role of science in influencing the views and decisions of lawmakers, and the role of the media in communicating the nature, magnitude, and source of the infection. We discovered the disturbing degree to which government and Big Tech are intertwined. This cast a troubling light on the role of trust, technology, and the rule of law—especially in emerging democracies.

It became clear that the relative success of Far Eastern countries in restricting the spread of the contagion could be explained by their greater acceptance of digital technologies, and their capacity and readiness to learn from their mistakes. On the other hand, it emerged that Western nations exhibited a reluctance to exploit the social and technological achievements of which we are so proud. This, we believe, is unrelated to the different values between East and West. In fact, it was the application of liberal democratic values—transparency, accountability, trust, and so on—that accounted for

Preface vii

the success of Taiwan and South Korea in keeping infections at bay, even if it required the enforcement of intrusive surveillance of the population. This is fundamental to the pages that follow. We repudiate the idea that fundamental rights are *per se* hostile to the public interest. We recognize that in a genuine crisis the curtailment of liberty may be a last resort. But such infringements of individual freedom can only be embarked upon when the principles of the rule of law are rigorously applied.

We are vexed by the kneejerk reaction to the use of personal information necessary to contact and trace infected individuals. Similarly, the alarm expressed in response to alleged 'censorship' of free speech cannot be legitimately generalized across the board. We have devoted most of our academic, professional, and activist lives to the protection of fundamental rights; nevertheless, they cannot be considered sacrosanct, particularly when lives and livelihoods are at stake.

Despite the extraordinary circumstances under which this book was written, produced, and published, Aakash Chakrabarty and Brinda Sen of Routledge provided friendly and cheerful support throughout. Thanks too to Keith Arnold for overseeing the production process.

AM
RW
10 October 2020

Acknowledgements

I wish once again to remember my mentor, the late Giancarlo Livraghi. A world-renowned advertising man, he devoted his life to the defence of freedom and justice. I also want to thank members of the academic and legal community who helped to elucidate the concepts that made this book possible. These include Giampiero Di Plinio and Beth Fairfield of d'Annunzio University, Hiroshi Miyashita of Chuo Daigaku, Giovanni Boniolo of the University of Ferrara, Francesco Vissani of the Gran Sasso Science Institute, Ross Anderson of the University of Cambridge, Giorgio Fabio Colombo of Nagoya University and Andrea Ortolani of Keio University, Bogdan Manolea of the Romanian digital rights NGO Asociația pentru Tehnologie și Internet. Rechtsanwalt and data protection expert, Axel Spies provided invaluable insights into the German constitutional system, and Maurizio Codogno, with his expertise in mathematics and physics, helped to clarify the (lack of)logic in the way the statistics of the pandemic have been misused by the media.

Andrea Monti

1 Confronting contagion

> Memory is an active process. Details have to be rehearsed to be retained, but who wants to rehearse the details of a pandemic? A war has a victor ... but a pandemic has only vanquished.
>
> Laura Spinney[1]

The velocity at which we now live—thanks, in large part, to the Internet—has changed the world forever. We not only communicate and transact business online in the blink of an eye; our very persona is shaped by social media. The almost instantaneous gratification of our needs and expectations has become a helter-skelter from which there is no going back. Fortunes are made or lost in stock market seconds; logistics transport goods across continents in days, if not hours. Even death wields its grim sickle at high speed: remotely controlled weapons and ordnance enable war to be waged swiftly and without the need for the loss of human 'boots on the ground'. Pace is all. The centrifugal rapidity of life without seat belts is the norm in most of the developed world.

Enter COVID-19. The brakes are suddenly applied. Governments across the globe enforce a lockdown as the response to the crisis, and we are cast into a vortex of fear and uncertainty.

Many of the challenges posed by the virus arise less from the disease than the reactions of policymakers and the fragility of the globalized industrial, economic, and financial infrastructure that, like Atlas, supports the world on its shoulders. The death toll and the stagnation of the economy are plain enough, but the pandemic has generated a range of other harms that are often obscured by the flashing lights of vehicles carrying victims to their fate.

In pursuit of a quick solution—a fundamentally political necessity—there has been a problematic attitude by certain governments toward the rule of law. By curtailing individual liberty in the ostensible defence of public health, they have diluted a number of civil rights. Italy, for instance, has issued a plethora of regulations that raise several basic constitutional

---

1 Spinney 2017.

2 Confronting contagion

questions. Germany, on the other hand, has resisted issuing special regulations, managing to maintain the protection of rights guaranteed in the constitution. The United Kingdom government has encountered some obstacles in the path of the introduction of Draconian measures thanks to the traditional British resilience against inroads into individual freedom. Nor did the United States resort to the President's executive powers, instead allowing state governors to resolve local problems. India permitted the police to compel compliance by the use of violence. China adopted its normal strategy: either 'Confucian' acquiescence or, as a backup, coercion. Japan has relied upon strong individual respect toward a central authority that does not need its power to be asserted. Taiwan and South Korea capitalized on their tragic experience of the outbreak of SARS in 2003 and MERS in 2015 by deploying an impressive technological and organizational response to the virus. Some 'third world' countries, Thailand, Vietnam, Senegal, and the Indian state of Kerala, succeeded in containing the virus without the need for digital contact tracing, artificial intelligence, or other advanced software technology.

The irrational, if understandable, fear of the virus engendered a blame game in which the principal target is China, which is accused of a number of transgressions, including covering up the outbreak and its extent, and the use of totalitarian policies to stem the epidemic. But similar objections have also been levelled at Western societies whose governments have been charged with adopting the tactics of a police state or pursuing an anti-scientific public policy approach. These exaggerated claims have not been especially constructive.

Western governments have from time to time adulterated the rule of law. But its status as a defining feature of a democratic society is rarely questioned. Even in the dark days following the 9/11 terrorist outrage or during the 'war on terror', or the Syrian and other North Africa and Middle East geopolitical crises its power endured. The present pandemic has, by contrast, produced a disconcerting indifference toward constitutional principles, which have been portrayed as legalistic pedantry that thwarts governments from doing 'the right thing'. As a consequence, the watchdog roles of citizens and civil liberties groups have often been hamstrung. In many countries politicians have found it expedient to conceal their decisions by invoking the talisman of public safety or emergency or by deferring to scientific 'experts'.

COVID-19 has not only dislocated the social contract between citizen and State, but also among citizens themselves. The sight of supermarkets' empty shelves and of anxious shoppers stockpiling food and other essentials has become routine across the world.[2] Wealth-based differences have

---

2 Panic buying in the United States has, however, extended to the purchase of guns and ammunition!

become starker and social rage has increased, fuelled by extremist political groups both within and outside legislatures. The zombie metaphor of George Romero's *Night of the Living Dead* was a prescient foretaste of the world we now inhabit:

> In his 1968 film, the zombies are a literal mass movement—a heaving, flesh-eating horde that up-ends the cosy, natural order of American society. One of the most its most startling scenes involves an undead daughter murdering its mother with a trowel; one generation suddenly turns on the other. The climactic scenes throw up an even more disturbing suggestion: as the small army of red necks roam the countryside, apparently enjoying the task of indiscriminately blasting everything they see, Romero strongly implies that the posse of shooters are little more than zombies themselves.[3]

Hobbes' *bellum omnium contra omnes*[4] obliges us to reconsider the relationship between the rule of law and power, between freedom and security, and the role of ignorance-induced fear and its effect on the political agenda.

Surviving COVID

Among the dramatic challenges to stability and security, pandemics rank alongside war, revolution, and famine. Governments faced with the pervasive uncertainty and fear generated by threats to tranquillity requires not only firm leadership, but the clear determination of public policy and effective strategies to manage and overcome the crisis. Almost no nation has been spared the devastating effects Coronavirus has wreaked on lives, livelihoods, and economies. The social, political, and national security consequences of the pandemic are the chief focus of this work.

Toward the end of 2019 an individual in the notorious Huanan seafood market in Wuhan was reportedly infected with a virus that apparently emanated from an animal. The virus—later identified as COVID-19—spread across the globe infecting about 30 million people and causing (or contributing to) the death of about 950,000 at the time of writing. So-called 'wet' markets (which are more accurately described as wildlife markets) are common in China. The Huanan market has a section selling wild animals including badgers, wolf pups, snakes, bamboo rats, and porcupines, mostly kept cruelly in tiny cages with no apparent concern for their suffering. One stall offered about a hundred varieties of live animals ranging from foxes to peacocks to masked palm civets; the last-mentioned creature is regarded as instrumental in transferring the SARS virus from bats to humans in the

3 Lambie 2019.
4 Hobbes 1647: 4.

4   Confronting contagion

2002/3 epidemic.[5] It has been reported that, as a result of the virus, China will ban the consumption of wild animals and clamp down on the illegal wildlife trade. According to a recent decision of the Standing Committee of the National People's Congress it will—supposedly—completely ban the eating of wild animals and clamp down on the illegal wildlife trade before legislation is amended to protect health and ecological security.[6]

Although the World Health Organization published a warning on 31 December 2019, and early cases had been identified since 11 January 2020, the West waited until the end of February or in some cases as late as mid-March before acknowledging the seriousness of the situation and taking action.[7] By contrast, several other countries, especially in Asia, such as Taiwan, activated their disease control system as early as 5 January 2020:

> On December 31, 2019, when the World Health Organization was notified of pneumonia of unknown cause in Wuhan, China, Taiwanese officials began to board planes and assess passengers on direct flights from Wuhan for fever and pneumonia symptoms before passengers could deplane. As early as January 5, 2020, notification was expanded to include any individual who had traveled to Wuhan in the past 14 days and had a fever or symptoms of upper respiratory tract infection at the point of entry ... On January 20, while sporadic cases were reported from China, the Taiwan Centers for Disease Control (CDC) officially activated the CECC for severe special infectious pneumonia under NHCC, with the minister of health and welfare as the designated commander.[8]

The manner in which different governments responded to the emergence of the disease made a significant difference to the death toll and the social fallout. There has been—inevitably—a parallel drawn between this disaster and previous pandemics, particularly the Spanish flu of 1918 which is estimated

---

5 It has been suggested that an intermediary host between bats and humans may be the pangolin which is described by the International Union for the Conservation of Nature as 'the most illegally traded mammal in the world'. www.iucn.org/commissions/ssc-groups/mammals/specialist-groups-f-z/pangolin (Visited 22 April 2020). They are prized for their meat and the alleged medicinal properties of their scales. According to an article in *Nature*, pangolins were not listed as being sold in Wuhan, although this may be because their sale is unlawful. www.nature.com/articles/d41586-020-00364-2 (Visited 22 April 2020).

6 *China Daily*, 24 February 2020. See too 'Shenzhen becomes first Chinese city to ban eating cats and dogs' *BBC News*. www.bbc.co.uk/news/world-asia-china-52131940 (Visited 22 April 2020).

7 Schumaker, Erin. 'Timeline: How coronavirus got started', *ABC News*, 23 April 2020. https://abcnews.go.com/Health/timeline-coronavirus-started/story?id=69435165 (Visited 15 May 2020).

8 Wang, Jason, Ng, Chun, Brook, Robert. 2020. Response to COVID-19 in Taiwan. JAMA. 2020; 323(14): 1341–1342. doi:10.1001/jama.2020.3151.

Confronting contagion 5

to have infected about 500 million people or a third of the world's population. It ended the lives of at least 50 million people and generated a host of social and moral consequences:

> Eugenics was a mainstream current of thought both before and after the 1918 flu, but the pandemic undermined it in at least one domain: infectious diseases. Previously, social Darwinist—and misguided—thinking about some human 'races' or castes being superior to others had mixed insidiously with the insight of Louis Pasteur and others that infectious diseases were preventable. They produced a toxic cocktail of an idea: people who caught infectious diseases only had themselves to blame.[9]

Radical changes in the political approach to public health occurred because of the realization that a pandemic requires action at a systemic rather than an individual level:

> It gave a big boost to the concept of socialized medicine and healthcare, which no country had really got around to organizing yet. The pandemic is what gave the stimulus to do that because there was a realization that a pandemic was a global health crisis you had to treat at the population level. You couldn't treat individuals and there was no point in blaming individuals for catching an illness or treating them in isolation. Russia was the first, followed by Western European nations, to put in place socialized healthcare systems. Along with that comes epidemiology, the search for patterns and causes and effects of patterns in healthcare. The baseline health of populations started to become much more transparent, and much more visible.[10]

A comparison with the Spanish flu[11] reveals common traits with the Coronavirus pandemic. The earlier devastating disease created xenophobia and superstition fuelled by ignorance, illiteracy, and war propaganda that was stringently censored by the State.[12] Although the 1918 experience contributed to the weakening of the then European great powers, it did not challenge the world's operational capabilities as COVID-19 has done.

Notwithstanding the relentless attempt of the media to increase the Coronavirus-attributed death count, at the time of writing the figures are considerably lower than other pandemics, including, of course, the Spanish

---

9 Spinney 2017. The Spanish flu emerged as the world was recovering from years of global war. It was to have some surprising and far-reaching effects, *BBC Future*, 17 October 2018. www.bbc.com/future/article/20181016-the-flu-that-transformed-the-20th-century (Visited 15 April 2020).
10 Whiting 2020.
11 See Jester, Uyeki, & Jernigan 2018; Kucharski 2020.
12 Whiting 2020.

6   Confronting contagion

flu. In fact, the manner in which COVID-19 assailed the world is more like the Antonine Plague of 165 AD (see below) that contributed to the disruption of the Roman Empire, and for very similar reasons:

> [T]he beginning of the 21st century looks like the time of Marcus Aurelius. In a world entirely and totally open to exchanges, connections, relationships, legitimate or not, the circulation of narratives has accelerated at a frightening pace, to the point where local cultures now exist only as very secondary resources for a kind of single market of fantasy on a global scale. The world is now a world of globalized and globalized cultures, and the circulation of narratives has accelerated at a frightening pace, to the point where local cultures now exist only as very secondary resources for a kind of single market of fantasy on a global scale. In this respect, the 21st century is beginning to look like the time of Marcus Aurelius.[13]

Unless this pandemic is swiftly resolved, and we look back on it as a period of collective global hysteria, it will be difficult not to acknowledge the reality that the pandemic exposed not only the economic frailty of an interconnected world but also nations' domestic differences in keeping communities united, in the extent to which the social contract was honoured, and in the setting of external limits to national geopolitical strategies. Policymakers need to construct a political and legal environment that facilitates a responsible and effective response to crises like a pandemic. This may require a reassessment of the existing legislative framework to ensure that any major obstacles to medical and social measures deployed to deal with the calamity are weakened or removed. Lawmakers and their advisers should resist the assumption that they are better placed than their citizens to calculate the costs and benefits of lockdowns. Moreover, local authorities are often better able to assess the impact of a shutdown on local businesses and community life.

Nationalism

But local solutions to crises are not an invitation to independence or secession. Independentism and nationalism have, of course, long been part of the history of numerous nations. Spain, the United Kingdom, Turkey, and India all contain powerful separatist parties and groups, along with several other nations. Prior to the pandemic, nations were somehow able to contain the centrifugal pressure. The virus, however, as was the case with its predecessors—the Imperial Roman Variola plague and the Spanish flu—has unleashed breakaway movements that undermine international stability.

13 Zylberman 2013: 29.

Confronting contagion 7

The current pandemic is a time of global uncertainty that may revamp social, economic and political models worldwide. Russia already faces the adverse consequences of the lockdown and oil price drop. But more may be to come. Personalist regimes like Putin's are based on a specific social contract: rights and freedoms in exchange for stability and welfare, especially in troubled times. What citizens and entrepreneurs see now is the state that fails to deliver and stays extremely tight-fisted towards businesses and those who lost their jobs. Instead, the president tells the regions to cope by themselves ... Should all this affect the stability of Putin's rule, should Moscow's grip over regions loosen, we might face another revival of regional autonomies and their attempts to regain the powers they once enjoyed.[14]

In Italy the restive ambitions of northern regions have becalmed, but local governors have exploited the pandemic to increase their autonomy by issuing regional ordinances in direct conflict with central government regulations and seizing de facto public security powers beyond their authority. In Hong Kong democracy protesters used the Coronavirus in their political struggle against Beijing, by demanding the Chief Executive to close the border with Mainland China. They did not, however, confine themselves to mere political action:

Beijing's increasing assertiveness in recent years has fueled outrage against perceived encroachment. It has also helped catalyze a distinct Hong Kong identity—one rooted in defending the territory's unique freedoms against an influx of mainland money, people and power. 'Hong Kong is not China' has become a rallying cry throughout the city, sprayed onto walls and chanted at protests. Anger extends to anything identified with China: emblems, businesses and even people. Long distrusted as agents of demographic, socioeconomic and even political occupation, mainlanders are now feared as vectors of disease, emboldening a bigotry that increasingly spills into violence.[15]

Nationalism found new strength in the pandemic both as a sort of last resort 'self-defence' and as a political strategy. During the peak of the contagion in the EU, countries reciprocally blocked the delivery of masks[16,17] overlooking the 'spirit of community' that is supposed to maintain harmony among member states.

14 Rogoża 2020.
15 Barron 2020.
16 Dahinten & Wabl 2020.
17 Tarquini 2020.

8 Confronting contagion

At the same time, notwithstanding declarations about the prospect of global availability of a cure, vaccine nationalism has arrived:

> In India … the Serum Institute signaled that, if development of the vaccine succeeds, most of the initial batches of vaccine will be distributed within India. … In March, the White House met with representatives from CureVac, a German biotech company developing a COVID-19 vaccine. The U.S. government is reported to have inquired about the possibility of securing exclusive rights over the vaccine. This prompted the German government to comment that 'Germany is not for sale'. Angela Merkel's chief of staff promptly stated that a vaccine developed in Germany had to be made available in 'Germany and the world' … U.S. and Russia, chose not to join the Access to COVID-19 Tools Accelerator, which was launched by the World Health Organization to promote collaboration among countries in the development and distribution of COVID-19 vaccines and treatments.[18]

Pandemics are a fact of life. Their containment is achieved principally by the establishment of early warning networks and rapid reaction task forces. Most countries have—at least on paper—accepted this approach. It was generally successful in the case of the SARS and MERS viruses (South Korea, for instance, did not succeed in managing MERS, but learned from its experience and succeeded in containing the Coronavirus outbreak).

Geopolitics

Pandemics also have an impact on geopolitics. Blame has been laid at the door of China by the United States and other countries, especially for intentionally delaying the existence of the Coronavirus. Iran has also been accused of refusing to accept the assistance of the United States[19] or of *Médecins Sans Frontières*[20] and its request (denied by the United States) for the lifting of economic sanctions on humanitarian grounds.[21] This poses the question whether under international humanitarian law there is a duty on sovereign States to keep health-related subjects outside of political tussles. Indeed, it is arguable that a violation of this obligation constitutes a crime against humanity. This is not as far-fetched as it may appear; a virus is a weapon,

---

18 Rutschman 2020.
19 Hafezi 2020.
20 *Médecins Sans Frontières* '"deeply surprised" that Iranian authorities put a stop to our COVID-19 response', 25 March 2020. www.msf.org/msf-surprised-iran-put-stop-our-covid-19-response (Visited 14 April 2020).
21 Fassihi 2020.

and weapons defend national security. It is no surprise that the Americans regard monitoring the disease in this light.[22]

> Hence the immense importance of safety issues, which sometimes affect sectors that no one in Europe would have the idea of placing under such sponsorship (education, hospitals, motorway facilities). On the contrary, when no security interests are at stake, the federal government's initiative gets bogged down: witness the failure, under Clinton, of the social security reform; witness again the extreme vulnerability of the health insurance reform wanted by Obama. The increase in the number of sectors subject to the security imperative represents a very serious challenge for the White House. It is therefore not surprising that Washington's growing power over research in the fight against epidemics and public health, which are a priori not very political, is now crucial elements of biodefense.[23]

Restricting rights

Treating a pandemic in this way inevitably raises the traditional argument about the extent to which fundamental rights can legitimately be curtailed to protect national security:

> The necessity of maintaining the public's trust also means that the argument that, in a public health emergency, there must be a trade-off between effective public health measures and civil rights is simply wrong. As the AIDS epidemic has demonstrated, the promotion of human rights can be essential for dealing effectively with an epidemic. Early in the course of the AIDS epidemic, public health officials recognized that mandatory screening for human immunodeficiency virus would simply help drive the epidemic underground, where it would spread faster and wider. Likewise, draconian quarantine measures would probably have the unintended effect of encouraging people to avoid public health officials and physicians rather than to seek them out. In this regard, the protection of civil liberties is a core ingredient in a successful response to a bioterrorist attack. Provisions that treat citizens as the enemy, with the use of the police for enforcement, are much more likely to cost lives than to save them.[24]

Apprehensive individuals are naturally more willing to tolerate limitations on their liberty if they believe such restrictions are likely to achieve their purpose. This may include the tracking of movement, compulsory medical

---

22 Markowitz & Rosner 2013.
23 Zylberman 2013: 252.
24 Annas 2002.

10 Confronting contagion

treatment, involuntary quarantine, restrictions on travel and the freedom of assembly, censorship of what the authorities regard as disinformation, the suspension of habeas corpus, and the policing of civilians, even by the military. Similarly, they will accept the move to an Internet-powered world of education, entertainment, sport, and so on, as well as the relocation of life and work from public to private places.

It has been suggested that in authoritarian societies there is a greater willingness to impose stringent quarantine and other restrictive measures than in open, liberal nations which rely on socially oriented measures such as managing an effective public health infrastructure and personal responsibility. 'Variations in prophylactic strategies are therefore the product of politics, the nature of the regimes, as well as the circumstances surrounding the spread of contamination'.[25]

> For nations that share the central values of a liberal democracy, safeguards of individual rights must bound the precautionary principle ... When taken together, the precautionary principle, the least intrusive/restrictive alternative, justice, and transparency underscore the importance of using voluntary rather than coercive measures whenever possible. Although mandatory measures and recourse to coercion may be necessary, efforts designed to elicit the voluntary cooperation of those at risk of acquiring or transmitting infectious diseases are preferable. Mass persuasion and public education to prevent panic and encourage risk avoidance are thus essential features of public health.[26]

On the face of it, it does appear to be the case that the more socially (although not necessarily socialist) inclined countries such those in Central and Northern Europe sought to minimize limitations on civil rights. By contrast, other countries with less affable feelings toward their people—China springs to mind—entrusted the police with extensive powers to control the populace by heavy-handed means when required. But this simple dichotomy does not account for other explanations for the use of stringent measures including, for example, an indifferent or underfunded health service or its limited capability to handle a pandemic. Italy is a paradigmatic case, with its public health system's efficiency reduced to a critical level, pandemic emergency plans were ready on paper but were never rehearsed or put into practice. Moreover, although the country can hardly be considered authoritarian, its longstanding economic and political crisis led to the enforcement of police-state-like measures rather than to a more 'civil' approach. The absence of trust in the authorities as well as the lack of transparency in formulating and communicating public policy combined to dictate the imposition of rigid measures.

25 Zylberman 2013: 415.
26 Gostin, Bayer, & Fairchild 2004.

Confronting contagion   11

This is closely related to another consequence peculiar to COVID-19: the relationship between the law, rights, and economics. A relentless slogan throughout the lockdown was 'we cannot allow the economy to shut down'. Thus, despite the noble assertion that a price tag cannot be put on lives, the reality is that our globalized economic and financial system left governments with a very limited set of options; all they could do was gradually to resume economic activity and reopen external borders as soon as possible. Nevertheless, the devastation suffered by the industrial and commercial sectors such as airlines, tourism, and vehicle manufacture speak volumes about the weaknesses exposed—rather than necessarily caused—by the pandemic.

While there is general consensus that we have little choice but to restrict rights (particularly freedom of assembly, movement, and privacy) in order to contain the virus, there is also a need to re-evaluate our globalized economic order that, in pursuit of profit, creates gross disparities between rich and poor, and endangers the planet. The pandemic has unavoidably cost millions of jobs and affected countless lives and livelihoods. The pandemic has also exposed disturbing trends in policymaking. Politicians either assigned their choices to scientists and 'experts', or used them as lightning rods to justify their decisions. In other cases—such as in the 'dialectic' between President Trump and leading virologist, Anthony Fauci—technical advice that does not accord with political strategy is adopted with considerable resistance.

The expanding role of executive power caused by the pandemic is a universal concern. Countries with a more robust democratic tradition can resort to Draconian measures without becoming authoritarian regimes. But those with an elastic notion of the separation of powers may seize the chance to weaken parliamentary oversight of their work. One must nevertheless concede that, under lockdown, it is not easy for parliamentarians physically to gather to enact by a majority the legislation or regulations. This has inflicted a wound on normal decision-making procedures:

> Faced with unprecedented disruption to the decision-making machinery of government—including travel bans and social-distancing restrictions on large meetings—officials in capitals worldwide have scrambled to adopt new working methods, including meetings by videoconference, and remote voting by ministers and parliaments ... Around the world, other governments are already taking extraordinary steps—some of which could permanently alter how those in power take decisions, hastening the acceptance of new technologies previously regarded as insecure or inappropriate for official business.[27]

Perhaps we have granted Big Tech and telecommunications companies the power to control the way institutions operate. This is a pertinent question

---

27 Herszernhorn 2020.

12 *Confronting contagion*

because these corporations that control information and communication technology are essentially based in the United States or—in the case of hardware—in China or in those countries hosting Chinese outsourcers that manufacture these products on behalf of the United States. Private social networking and search engine enterprises have acquired a de facto power to decide what we can say, read, and listen to, usurping, at least in the West, real political power. Another related problem is the public enforcement of the provisions against the circulation of information that is perceived to imperil peace and security. The line between genuine threats to public order and the freedom of expression has often been blurred during the pandemic. Ultimately it is a matter for the judiciary, but the emergency has significantly reduced the effectiveness of the courts.

The crisis raises a plethora of other social, economic, and political issues—several of which are considered in the following chapters. It is clear that there is an urgent need for an international coordinated effort:

> Potentially devastating increases in economic inequality, unemployment, debt, and poverty, as well as pressures on the stability of financial institutions, will put enormous strains on governance systems of all types ... Amid a new crisis even more daunting in scale, there is a natural tendency for governments and individuals alike to be consumed by the urgency of near-term domestic fallout from the pandemic. But just as the virus's contagion respects no borders, its political effects will inevitably sweep across boundaries and continue to echo long after the health emergency has eased.[28]

Digital technology has been vital in containing the virus and its social consequences. Western democracies, suffocated by a ubiquitous 'precaution principle', have failed to encourage the social acceptance of information technology and of the technology of information (the difference is revealed in Chapter 4). There has also been a reluctance to acknowledge the success of Far Eastern countries in combatting the virus:

> [I]t could be that East Asian democracies have a kind of 'authoritarian residue' that has helped in the initial response to this crisis. South Korea and Taiwan are certainly vibrant democracies—but they are also relatively new democracies compared to many in Europe. As a result, citizens may have a different relationship with the state and be more willing to accept sudden restrictions of freedoms ... There may now be difficult trade-offs to be made between those basic rights and security—and, after the experience of coronavirus, many citizens may choose security ... Even before the coronavirus hit, there was already much discussion

28 Brwon, Brechenmacher, & Carothers 2020.

Confronting contagion 13

of a crisis of liberal democracy ... In particular, 'illiberal democracies' seemed to be emerging in many places including Europe ... This model of 'illiberal democracy'—in other words, one in which elections continue to be held but some individual rights are curtailed—may emerge stronger from this new crisis.[29]

'Illiberal democracies' (a geopolitical oxymoron) are not new. Like the influenza virus, they are always around, and, when the moment is appropriate, they spread around the globe.

A detailed discussion of these questions is beyond the scope of this book, but we reflect upon the impact of the most striking instances in the pages that follow.

References

Annas, George. 2002. 'Bioterrorism, Public Health, and Civil Liberties' *New England Journal of Medicine*, DOI: 10.1056/NEJM200204253461722 : www.nejm.org/doi/full/10.1056/NEJM200204253461722 (Visited 18 September 2020).

Barron, Laignee. 2020. 'The Coronavirus Has Brought Out the Ugly Side of Hong Kong's Protest Movement'. *Time*, online edition, 19 February. https://time.com/5784258/hong-kong-democracy-separatism-coronavirus-covid-19/ (Visited 15 March 2020).

Brwon, Frances, Brechenmacher, Saskia, Carothers, Thomas. 2020. 'How Will the Coronavirus Reshape Democracy and Governance Globally?'. *Carnegie Endowment for International Peace*, 6 April. https://carnegieendowment.org/2020/04/06/how-will-coronavirus-reshape-democracy-and-governance-globally-pub-81470 (Visited 14 May 2020).

Dahinten, Jan, Wabl, Matthias. 2020. 'Germany Faces Backlash From Neighbors Over Mask Export Ban'. *Bloomberg News*, 9 March. www.bloomberg.com/news/articles/2020-03-09/germany-faces-backlash-from-neighbors-over-mask-export-ban (Visited 18 April 2020). doi:10.1056/NEJM200204253461722.

Gostin, Lawrence, Bayer, Ronald, Fairchild, Amy. 2004. 'Ethical and Legal Challenges Posed by Severe Acute Respiratory Syndrome: Implications for the Control of Severe Infectious Disease Threats'. *Journal of the American Medical Association*, 290(24): 3229–3237. doi:10.1001/jama.290.24.3229.

Hafezi, Parisa. 2020. 'Iran's Khamenei Rejects U.S. Help Offer, Vows to Defeat Coronavirus'. *Reuters World News*, online edition, April. www.reuters.com/article/us-health-coronavirus-iran/irans-khamenei-rejects-u-s-help-offer-vows-to-defeat-coronavirus-idUSKBN21909Y15.

Herszernhorn, David. 2020. 'Democracy in Critical Care as Coronavirus Disrupts Governments'. *Politico*, online edition, 24 March. www.politico.eu/article/democracy-in-critical-care-as-coronavirus-disrupts-governments/ (Visited 14 May 2020).

Hobbes, Thomas. 1647. *De Cive*. Amsterdam: L. Elzevirium.

---

29 Kundnani 2020.

14 *Confronting contagion*

Jester, B., Uyeki, T., Jernigan, D. 2018. 'Readiness for Responding to a Severe Pandemic 100 Years After 1918'. *American Journal of Epidemiology*, 187: 2596. https://doi.org/10.1093/aje/kwy165.

Kucharski, Adam. 2020. *The Rules of Contagion: Why Things Spread—and Why They Stop*. London: Profile.

Kundnani, Hans. 2020. 'Coronavirus and the Future of Democracy in Europe'. *Chatham House Expert Comment*, 31 March. www.chathamhouse.org/expert/comment/coronavirus-and-future-democracy-europe (Visited 19 April 2020).

Lambie, Ryan. 2019. 'George Romero and the Meanings of his Zombies: Den of geeks'. 5 February. www.denofgeek.com/movies/george-romero-zombies-exp lained/ (Visited 19 March 2020).

Markowitz, Gerald, Rosner, David. 2013. *Are We Ready? Public Health Since 9/11*. Berkeley: University of California Press.

Rogoża, Jadwiga. 2020. 'Russia: Can Covid-19 Help Reinstate Kaliningrad's Autonomy?'. www.ispionline.it/it/pubblicazione/russia-can-covid-19-help-reins tate-kaliningrads-autonomy-26222 (Visited 17 July 2020).

Rutschman, Ana Santos. 2020. 'How "Vaccine Nationalism" Could Block Vulnerable Populations Access to COVID-19 Vaccines'. *The Conversation*, 17 June. https ://theconversation.com/how-vaccine-nationalism-could-block-vulnerable-popul ations-access-to-covid-19-vaccines-140689 (Visited 19 July 2020).

Schumaker, Erin. 2020. 'Timeline: How Coronavirus Got Started'. *ABC News*, 23 April. https://abcnews.go.com/Health/timeline-coronavirus-started/story? id=69435165 (Visited 15 May 2020).

Spinney, Laura. 2017. *Pale Rider: The Spanish Flu of 1918 and How It Changed the World*. New York: Vintage.

Tarquini, Andrea. 2020. 'Coronavirus, Mascherine per l'Italia Sequestrate Dalla Repubblica Ceca. L'ambasciata Italiana: "Praga si è Impegnata a Inviarci un Numero Uguale"'. Repubblica.it, online edition, 21 March. www.repubblica. it/esteri/2020/03/21/news/coronavirus_cosi_la_repubblica_ceca_ha_sequestrat o_680_mila_mascherine_inviate_dalla_cina_all_italia-251883320/ (Visited 18 April 2020).

Wang, Jason, Ng, Chun, Brook, Robert. 2020. 'Response to COVID-19 in Taiwan'. *Journal of the American Medical Association*, 23(14): 1341–1342. doi:10.1001/jama.2020.3151.

Whiting, Kate. 2020. 'A Science Journalist Explains How the Spanish Flu Changed the World'. *World Economic Forum Agenda*, 30 April. www.weforum.org/agen da/2020/04/covid-19-how-spanish-flu-changed-world/ (Visited 14 May 2020).

Zylberman, Patrick. 2013. *Tempêtes Microbiennes (NRF Essais)*. Paris: Editions Gallimard.

2 Science and power

> We should manage our Fortune as our Constitution; enjoy it when good, have Patience when 'tis bad, and never apply violent Remedies but in Cases of Necessity.[1]

Few clichés ring as true as that which maintains that knowledge is power. The acquisition and control of information—and precluding others from obtaining it—have always been fundamental to the exercise of political authority. Whether it is scientific knowledge that enabled the United States to gain the atomic supremacy that ended the Second World War,[2] the sophisticated psycho-sociological experiments of Nazi Germany's propaganda,[3] Stalinist Russia's дезинформация,[4] or the chicanery of Voodoo practitioners,[5] information is the quintessence of control.

Such knowledge extends to science and technology in the pursuit of political power whether it is used to impose control through fear or, in more open societies, to shape public opinion through more subtle means: propaganda and persuasion. The relationship between science and power, or, more specifically, between scientists and politicians, has been a fundamental element in the COVID-19 pandemic. The role of scientific advisers has been at the heart of the formulation, design, application, and enforcement of public policy. It has shaken conventional assumptions about the already problematic relationship between citizens and their rights, and government.

In contrast to security threats, such as terrorist attacks whose impact on civil liberties, as paradoxical as it may seem, is limited, safety concerns generated by the encounter with an invisible and ubiquitous pathogenic agent has resulted in a generally quiescent public willing to tolerate significant restrictions of traditional freedoms. The metaphor of war has been widely,

---

1 François de la Roche Foucault 1749: 69.
2 Krige 2014: 229.
3 Welch 1993: 1–15.
4 Hazan 2017.
5 Del Guercio 1986.

16   *Science and power*

but inappropriately, used to describe the pandemic. In times of war, it is (relatively) easy to rationalize being on the receiving end of carpet bombing,or to accept the scarcity of goods, and still maintain even partial respect for consideration of individual rights. But facing an invisible, non-human threat is different: there is nobody with whom to negotiate, and no place to hide.

This reduced sensitivity to the need to preserve many of the democratic achievements of Western society is vividly illustrated by the debate about the tracking and tracing every individual spreader of the virus, and especially by the contact tracing software platforms. Such discourse inevitably descends into a hollow balancing exercise between 'privacy' and 'security', as both sides invoke 'science' to support their respective claims. In order to understand the role played by COVID-19 in the reshaping of the public policy process it is necessary to consider its relationship with science and those disciplines that purport to adopt the scientific method.

What is public policy?

At its core, public policy is the epi-phenomenon of power. It defines the political goals of those who exercise power through the instrument of public policies. In simple terms, 'ruling is an assertion of the will, an attempt to exercise control, to shape the world. Public policies are instruments of this assertive ambition'.[6] The dynamic of power and its relationship to public policy is well expressed by Eric Liu:

> There are six main sources of civic power. First, there's physical force and a capacity for violence ... A second core source of power is wealth. Money creates the ability to buy results and to buy almost any other kind of power. The third form of power is state action, government. This is the use of law and bureaucracy to compel people to do or not do certain things ... The fourth type of power is social norms ... Norms don't have the centralized machinery of government. They operate in a softer way, peer to peer ... The fifth form of power is ideas. An idea ... can generate boundless amounts of power if it motivates enough people to change their thinking and actions. And so the sixth source of power is numbers, lots of humans. A vocal mass of people creates power by expressing collective intensity of interest and by asserting legitimacy.[7]

From the perspective of sovereign power, this translates into the attribution to the State of a series of prerogatives: the use of force by way of the army and law enforcement authorities (the monopoly of coercive power), the exclusive ownership of legal tender and control over the economic and

---

6 Moran, Rein, & Goodin 2008: 3.
7 Liu 2014.

financial systems (control over wealth creation mechanisms), the ability to create rules and procedures as the only way for a citizen to interact with the State's public administration (law and bureaucracy). In short, public policies constitute the 'proceduralization' of power or, as Liu succinctly puts it, 'policy is power frozen'.[8] Customs and ideas, on the other hand, generate a 'social drive' turning the masses into a social golem controlled by the succeeding leader; they are the floating parts that, according to their orientation, distinguish a democratic State from a tyranny.

In the West, over the centuries, from the various monotheisms to the secular religions such as Marxism and liberalism, the imposition of State-created customs and ideology clashed with 'libertarian' views inspired by 'new' ideas from religious creeds and political theories. Occasionally it heralded the (mostly) peaceful entrance into parliament of a new political party (e.g., the rise of communism in Italy after WWII). But it also produced the less pacific advent of events such as the French *la Terreur* or the 1917 Bolshevik *coup* in Russia. Democratic principles were sacrificed at an enormous human cost. In Asia, Confucianism achieved acquiescence to State-defined values by imposing, through a complex system of rituals and moral tenets, an approach that, despite local differences, extended to other Asian countries such as Korea, Vietnam, and Japan that either developed their own version or eventually discarded this pervasive cultural influence. In India, the inextricable knot of philosophy, religion, social structure, and politics was tied together by Hinduism's caste system and by the complex philosophical concept of *Dharma*[9] which is 'the moral order of the universe and a code of living that embodies the fundamental principles of law, religion, and duty that governs all reality'.[10]

The translation of *Dharma* into social and, later, legal constructs (the latter documented in the ponderous *History of Dharmaśāstra*[11]) was the core of precept-abiding compliance in India. It is not State-imposed, but represents an essential part of the creed of social groups and individuals; it thus demonstrates a powerful resilience to social change. Notwithstanding the formal abolition of the caste system in 1950 *Dharma* and the caste system continue to be a major element of social control[12] and an obstacle to the secularization of modern India.

---

8 Liu ibid.
9 Harvard Divinity School, *The Religious Literacy Project, Dharma: The Social Order*. https ://rlp.hds.harvard.edu/religions/hinduism/dharma-social-order (Visited 9 April 2020).
10 Berkeley Center for Religion, Peace & World Affairs, *Dharma (Hinduism)*, Georgetown University. https://berkleycenter.georgetown.edu/essays/dharma-hinduism (Visited 9 April 2020).
11 Pandurang 1930–1962.
12 Ravi 2016.

18   Science and power

Power (whether political, social, or religious)[13] is reluctant to accept whatever limits its freedom of action. Nevertheless, the complexity of society contains institutional and social checks and balances that constrain or at least limit the exercise of untrammelled power. This was the case even in the Middle Ages when *Magna Carta* restricted for the first time the power of the king, subjecting him to the law and, before that, when Rome ruled the world, even the powerful Roman Republic's patricians, to maintain their authority, were required to stipulate with plebeians the concession in the form of *tribunicia potestas.*

The king's intolerance of any hindrance to his will, or caprice, is brilliantly captured in *Gorgias*, Plato's dialogue in which Socrates defeats the young rhetorician, Callicles, by opposing a prescient notion of the rule of law that was disliked by the Sophists who espoused the idea that laws were the instruments by which the weak prevented the strong from ruling according to their wishes. Later, in 66 BC, Cicero's closing argument in the *Pro Cluentio* powerfully reinforced the importance of the rule of law with his iconic statement, *legum servi sumus, ut liberi esse possimus*: we serve the law so that we can be free.

Reading the past through the lens of 'fundamental rights'—a relatively recent Western concept—would be methodologically unsound, for, to return to the examples just mentioned, neither the *tribunicia potestas* nor the *Magna Carta* or the French Revolution could be described as movements propelled by ordinary people. It is, however, worth remarking that (unless the other party was unwilling to negotiate), the law was the tool used by the opposing sides to smooth rough angles or as a shield to preserve an aura of legitimacy as in the case of the Japanese 幕府[14] or when 'puppet' rulers were imposed by foreign powers, as occurred with last Chinese emperor 溥儀, who became the ruler of the puppet-state of Manchukuo.[15]

The survival of the Indian caste system despite its abolition by law is a paradigmatic example of the fact that public policies, whether by legislative reform or as an economic strategy or whatever else serves the exercise of power, are effective as soon as there is general acceptance by citizens.

---

13 Max Weber's explanation of why people believe they are obliged to obey the law is instructive. It leads him to draw his famous distinction between three types of legitimate domination: *traditional* (where 'legitimacy is claimed for it and believed in by sanctity of age-old rules and powers'), *charismatic* (based on 'devotion to the exceptional sanctity, heroism or exemplary character of an individual person'), and *legal-rational* domination (which rests on 'a belief in the legality of enacted rules and the right of those elevated to authority under such rules to issue commands'). See Weber 1951; 1954. For a brief account of Weber's theory of law and legitimate domination, see Wacks 2020; Ch 7.

14 幕府 (Bakufu) stands for 'tent government' and identifies the military power of the 征夷大将軍 (Sei-i Taishōgun) that, in practice, ruled Japan from 1185 to 1868. See Hisho 1912: 83.

15 See Young 1999.

Policy and persuasion

Without wide support, the only way to secure compliance is through the use of force that, as history demonstrates, cannot be applied at its maximum intensity for too long before it excites an adverse reaction from the people. This is why the pursuit of political goals requires at the outset the managing (or manufacturing) of citizens' consent and only later the mastering of the science of administrative techniques (economic planning, law-making, security management, health governance, and other aspects of governmental control).

Consent management—propaganda—is typically deployed by those in power to achieve their goals through a system of policies. To this end, the techniques to control public opinion have always been somewhat ingenuous (for instance, the timeless *panem et circenses* of Emperor Nero), but have improved over time. But these techniques have received a significant boost from the Internet and the online platforms that make traditional methods appear unsophisticated.[16] Public relations, advertising, and psychometrics (and all its nuances) are now complemented by consent-moulding methods similar to those employed in the information warfare's PsyOps: the psychological aspect of military operations practised by the Athenians, Romans, and theorized in 1531 by Niccolò Machiavelli:

> Deceiving in an ordinary course of action is detestable, still, it is commendable and glorious when waging war. Those who defeat the enemy by cheating should be praised like he who wins by might.[17]

PsyOps consist of different techniques, ranging from weakening the 'spirit' of enemy soldiers and the trust of civilians in their government, to a well-orchestrated campaign of mis- and disinformation involving the use of the mass media to obstruct the consent-management system of a given country. The ultimate consent management system is, of course, depicted in Orwell's *Nineteen Eighty-Four*, where Big Brother is proven to be persistently right by his absolute control over ideas and the behaviour of citizens. This is memorably described, at the very beginning of the book, when Winston Smith is attempting to hide from the 'telescreen':

> The telescreen received and transmitted simultaneously. Any sound that Winston made, above the level of a very low whisper, would be picked up by it; moreover, so long as he remained within the field of

---

16 See Monti & Wacks 2019: 68.

17 'Ancora che usare la fraude in ogni azione sia detestabile, nondimeno nel maneggiar la guerra è cosa laudabile e gloriosa, e parimenti è laudato colui che con fraude supera il nimico, come quello che lo supera con le forze'. Machiavelli, Niccolò *Discorsi sopra la Prima Deca di Tito* Livio, Book III, chapter 40. Milan: Sonzogno Editore, 286.

20 *Science and power*

vision which the metal plaque commanded, he could be seen as well as heard. There was of course no way of knowing whether you were being watched at any given moment. How often, or on what system, the Thought Police plugged in on any individual wire was guesswork. It was even conceivable that they watched everybody all the time. But at any rate they could plug in your wire whenever they wanted to. You had to live—did live, from habit that became instinct—in the assumption that every sound you made was overheard, and, except in darkness, every movement scrutinized.[18]

Ironically, Orwell had in mind the Stalinist USSR, and could probably never have imagined that his account was more akin to the ubiquitous search engines and social networking platforms now extensively used in the 'democratic West'. Direct and invasive controls are widely practised in countries with an 'elastic' understanding of the word 'democracy' that appears in their self-given name or description. In contrast, other enduring manipulative techniques (most of which are described by Edward Bernays,[19] Vance Packard,[20] and Noam Chomsky[21]) have been deployed in the 'free world' and are reaching new peaks of efficiency thanks to the ubiquity of media and information technology activities. The perennial goals of State propaganda (value engraving, polarization against 'the enemy', fear exploitation, and the manufacture of artificial needs) are still pursued but in a more subtle, and therefore barely detectable, manner. Chomsky identifies the phenomenon as follows:

> The American approach to social control is so much more sophisticated and pervasive that it deserves a new name. It is not propaganda any more, it's 'prop-agenda'. It's not so much the control of what we think, but the control of what we think about.[22]

This methodology had a wider heuristic value even outside the United States and further research has exposed the critical role of the media in setting the agenda for their own goals by spreading fear, uncertainty, and doubt not only in the context of military operations, but even in relation to United Nations' peacekeeping interventions and international affairs:

---

18 Orwell 1948: 3.
19 Bernays 1928.
20 Packard 1959.
21 Chomsky 1989.
22 Available at http://beevine.newsvine.com/_news/2007/08/14/895716-noam-chomsky-how-propaganda-works-in-the-west, now through the Web Archive Project at https://web.archive.org/web/20071027104635/http://beevine.newsvine.com/_news/2007/08/14/895716-noam-chomsky-how-propaganda-works-in-the-west (Visited 10 April 2020).

Fear—of crime, of flying, of war—is disproportionate to the realities. Whether manifesting itself in a 'fortress America' mentality, a British fear of the European Union or an EU fear of 'mad cow disease' from Britain, complicated issues are communicated to the public as if they were simple events, with very little media responsibility for those issues once they are no longer deemed 'newsworthy'. In this way the media set the popular agenda not so much in terms of telling the public what to think, but in prioritising what they should think about.[23]

The 'prop-agenda' is still practised, but it is now complemented, and perhaps surpassed, by what may be dubbed the 'nil-agenda'. This is the annihilation of the difference between 'right' and 'wrong' and the induced perception that having the right to express an idea renders it correct. All competing ideas thus carry the same 'truth' weight so it does not actually matter who (or what) is wrong or right because what matters is merely whose side I am on. This polarization is typical of social-networking flames where the contenders seek only to state their point of view rather than to become involved in a genuine conversation or discussion. From the perspective of those who wield political power, it is no longer necessary to 'convince' any-one to 'accept' or question a policy on its merits because a carefully written narrative can trigger a 'confirmation bias' in the targeted audience.

We consider below the impact of 'nudge theory'[24] whose application delayed both the United Kingdom and United States' assessment of the impact of COVID-19 and possibly contributed to a higher number of vic-tims. For present purposes, it is worth mentioning that this late reincarna-tion of behaviourism combined with the similar clinical psychotherapeutic theories on which the manipulative technique of neuro-linguistic program-ming (NLP) are built won recognition by politicians in some of the most powerful countries in the world. Nudge theory thus marks a decisive depar-ture from the idea that political goals, and the related policies, require the consent and support of the governed on the basis of facts rather than on evanescent sentiment or stimulus-response induced reaction.

Needless to say, since the dawn of time the emotion of a crowd and the ability to control it have played a crucial role in the formulation of impor-tant choices such as, for instance, the declaration of war.[25] Even the ancients knew how to tell a mere rhetorician from an authentic leader:

When Aeschines spoke,
Athenians said:
'How beautiful his talks'.

23 Taylor 1997: 194.
24 Thaler and Sunstein 2009.
25 See generally Riesman 1947.

22 *Science and power*

When Demosthenes called,
Athenians said:
'Let's unite against Philip'.[26]

Here the purpose is to convince people to buy a particular product rather than embrace political reform. Still, there is a difference between an honest communication meant to inform people and a set of manipulative strategies to secure blind acceptance of a softly spoken diktat, but a diktat nonetheless. Nevertheless, and this is a critical question for those who set political goals, we need to enquire whether honesty really matters in respect of shaping public opinion. A deluge of words and countless books have been dedicated to answering this question, but none better than Edward Bernays' balanced yet cynical grasp of reality:

> The conscious and intelligent manipulation of the organized habits and opinions of the masses is an important element in democratic society. Those who manipulate this unseen mechanism of society constitute an invisible government which is the true ruling power of our country ... We are governed, our minds are molded, our tastes formed, our ideas suggested, largely by men we have never heard of.[27]

Citizens, however, are not the only potential source of concern for the ruling power whose preservation relies upon the capability to keep the other cogs of law enforcement operating effectively rather than seizing the moment to work against it. A good example of this public policy conundrum is the emergence of a crisis, be it caused by war, natural disaster, or a pandemic. At an abstract level, the goal, for instance, of pandemic management collapses into a single line: saving as many lives as possible. The practical enforcement of this goal translates into measures to develop a vaccine, find a cure, protect public order and security, and manage the recovery of the country from economic catastrophe. For these measures to work, however, it is fundamental to ensure global compliance that can be achieved by appropriately exploiting social beliefs rather than a religion-based approach founded on orders issued by force of mere authority.

There are, nevertheless, other, less apparent, but equally pertinent, issues: the preservation of executive power from the threatening presence of the emergency entities established by law or created *ad hoc*, the possible

---

26 For about a decade this claim, whose final line was 'We belong to the school of Demosthenes', was an essential part of the advertising agency Livraghi, Ogilvy & Mather's identity and captures perfectly the role of emotion as a factor that drives decisions: stay away from smugness, narcissistic contemplation of our own work, and from its aesthetic or intellectual quality for its own sake, Livraghi 1998, 'La strategia'. www.gandalf.it/m/strat02.htm (Visited 9 April 2020).

27 Bernays: 9.

Science and power 23

attempts by the executive to drain power from parliament, the exploitation of the consequence of the pandemic to pursue geopolitical ambitions and seize or extend control over foreign countries. Emergencies, whether staged or arising from natural causes, provide an opportunity to alter or disrupt the balance of power, whether locally or globally. Moreover, and this is an issue peculiar to our times, the management of public policy in an emergency needs to take into account the high level of industrial, economic, and technological interconnection between States of different political persuasions.

Of course, business relationships have always been separated (at least on the public stage) from the official position of States and governments. The East India Company was supposed to be 'only' a private entity exploiting Indian resources, but in reality, it proved crucial in instituting and maintaining British rule in the country. IBM struck a strategic alliance with the Third Reich to sell electromechanical machines that facilitated the Holocaust.[28] Weapon systems and technology sales are a longstanding method by which to secure control over another State:

> If a country wants to acquire jet fighters, it has to be reasonably friendly with one of six countries: Sweden, the United States, France, the United Kingdom, China, or Russia. Once a deal is made, it will need to stay friendly, otherwise the flow of spare parts and ancillary equipment will stop.[29]

This strategy is more valid, the more sophisticated the technology that makes the weapons systems work, not only for the control that the manufacturing country exercises over logistics, personnel training and platform maintenance, but especially for the extreme dependence of these systems on computer components. In the case of the American F-35 jet fighter, for example, it uses the Autonomous Logistics Information System (ALIS) platform. Like the priests of the 'atomic churches' of the Foundation imagined by Isaac Asimov, therefore, those who control how the weapons operate, rather than the weapons themselves, wield the real power over their customers.

On the other hand, it is quite clear that it is not the sale of a few naval units or a small flock of helicopters that strengthens the defensive apparatus of a small country. The real advantage for the seller country is the availability of support points, or even bases, in case the need for tactical deployment in those areas arises.

For a long time, this method of influencing public policy was unilateral, as the States on the receiving end of the financial aid or technology had no way to 'fight back' for their autonomy. Hence the more influential countries were not at risk of being 'attacked' or otherwise threatened by

28 Black 2001.
29 Luttwak 2016: 31.

24 *Science and power*

their 'friends'. But there is change afoot. Even a superpower like the United States, let alone other less powerful countries, is not free to use its might at will both because of their industrial, economic, and financial dependence on China, and because of the return of Russia to the world geopolitical stage. While the cartwheel of globalized business spun undisturbed, criticism of the role of China as a 'universal factory' and 'global cash reserve', as well as of Vladimir Putin's crackdown on fundamental rights was sacrificed on the altar of financial profit. Now that the cartwheel has abruptly stopped, political leaders are falling over themselves to 'discover' that they neither have the strength nor the means to prevent Eastern superpowers from increasing their de facto power internationally.

This external influence on political goal-setting and their enforcement negatively alters the balance between policy, law, and rights in those countries lacking the strength to resist the pressure associated with financial and other forms of aid and support offered out of a sense of 'international friendship'. In the worst-case scenario, a country might de facto change sides, switching from its previous ally to a new one and entering into a different system of values, thus exposing the risk to freedom and fundamental rights that were won at great sacrifice in WWII. In view of this disquieting development, the role of public policy is transformed into overcoming the urge to use the emergency's needs to eliminate the checks and balances on power, and to reaffirm the centrality of the rule of law. This is a role that, as the COVID-19 emergency has dramatically demonstrated, has not always been exercised with sufficient vigour.

Playing God

As suggested above, from a public policy perspective every emergency places in the government's hands the same responsibility: deciding who dies. Nevertheless, during the pandemic, the media has given this question substantial coverage, as if it were a novel moral dilemma. It described the predicament of the ethical quandary of doctors in emergency care having to choose which patients deserve to be in the ICU, while consigning others to their fate[30] or, at a policy level, reporting politicians' bold claims about not wishing to put a price tag on human life[31] and asking whether or not managing the pandemic is reduced to a contest between human life and economic stability.[32]

But this is exactly what lies at the heart of politics and public policy. Every parliament, every government, and every international body encounters this very predicament whenever a budget is formulated that reduces

30 Montalto 2020.
31 Young 2020.
32 Paresky 2020.

access to the public health system, or when sanctions are imposed against a country resulting in death by disease or starvation in the name of the 'national interest'. During the pandemic, however, the media and politicians exploited this routine activity as if it were an ineluctable factor in determining whether a lockdown was justified despite its social and economic fallout. Hard choices—like the bombing of Hiroshima and Nagasaki—test the moral fibre of policymakers. President Truman expressed the problem in forthright terms:

> I know that Japan is a terribly cruel and uncivilized nation in warfare but I can't bring myself to believe that because they are beasts, we should ourselves act in that same manner. For myself I certainly regret the necessity of wiping out whole populations because of the 'pigheadedness' of the leaders of a nation, and, for your information, I am not going to do it unless absolutely necessary ... My object is to save as many American lives as possible but I also have a humane feeling for the women and children in Japan.[33]

Sometimes a choice is taken in spite of a reality check, and based upon a major error of strategic assessment. Marshal Badoglio was aware of the actual might of the Italian Armed Forces, therefore he tried to discourage Mussolini from joining the Germans in WWII. Dismissing Badoglio's concerns, the *Duce* replied, 'I tell you that by September everything will be concluded, and that I need a few thousand casualties so as to join the peace negotiation with the status of a belligerent'.[34] By the end of the war, however, 'a few thousand' actually numbered almost half a million, including civilians—and Italy was excluded from the famous photograph of the Yalta Big Three.

Machtpolitik, the politics of power, offers countless examples of how the ethical limitations of judgements about life and death can be activated or neglected in the struggle for domination. For example, an article entitled 'Did Xi Jinping Deliberately Sicken the World?' published by the Asia-focused journal, *The Diplomat*, suggests that the spread of the COVID-19 from China to the rest of the world might have been caused, and could have been alleviated, by the manner in which the country downplayed the extent of the virus, and by the desire to portray China as not being alone in suffering the consequences of the epidemic:

> Although the emergence of the novel coronavirus now known as SARS-CoV-2 was probably not due to China's actions, the emphasis that its authoritarian system places on hiding bad news likely gave the disease

---

33 Hasegawa 2005: 202.
34 Badoglio 1946: 37.

26 *Science and power*

a sizable head start infecting the world. But most ominously, China's obsession with image and *Machtpolitik* raises serious questions about its lack of moral limits … Why should China suffer the effects of a pandemic while others stayed safe—and increased their strength relative to China—based on China's own costly experience? [35]

The article describes this possibility as 'inimical to human decency'. Yet, in a classic example of *praeteritio*, it leaves the doubt in the reader's mind that China has a degree of culpability in the spreading of COVID-19. Whether this is a skirmish in the disinformation battle between China and the United States or a credible theory is irrelevant as it poses the question: how far can a sovereign power go in pursuit of its goals? An answer may be found in a debate in the British House of Commons during WWII. Two days before Winston Churchill was appointed Prime Minister, Robert Tatton Bower, a Royal Navy officer rebuffed his fellow MPs' vision of a 'gentlemanly' conduct of war, reminding them that 'when you are fighting for your life against a ruthless opponent you cannot be governed by the Queensberry rules'.[36] This hard-headed asseveration nicely echoes Von Clausewitz's warning:

> Kind-hearted people might of course think there was some ingenious way to disarm or defeat an enemy without too much bloodshed and might imagine this is the true goal of the art of war. Pleasant as it sounds, it is a fallacy that must be exposed; war is such a dangerous business that the mistakes which come from kindness are the very worst.[37]

Political expediency frequently determines the decision whether to save lives. When confronted with the opportunity to send a mercenary expeditionary force to end the genocide committed in various parts of the world, the United Nations refused to pursue the option because 'this solution is deemed unacceptable by the moral giants who run the United Nations. They claim that it is objectionable to employ—sniff—mercenaries. More objectionable, it seems, than passing empty resolutions, sending ineffectual peacekeeping forces and letting genocide continue'.[38]

Is the United Nations' decision a painful but necessary choice to prevent the resurgence of further instability in developing countries even at the huge cost of human lives, the outcome of a hypocritical Pilatesque attitude? Or it is a pragmatic assessment of the unfeasibility of a course of action?

---

35 Lowsen 2020.
36 Ridgen 2004: 1.
37 von Clausewitz 1984: 75.
38 Barnes 2016: 143.

When Kofi Annan was UN Undersecretary General for Peacekeeping, he explored the option of hiring the South African private military company Executive Outcomes to aid in the Rwandan refugee crisis. He ultimately decided against the option, declaring that 'the world is not yet ready to privatize peace'.[39]

Ideology, *Realpolitik*—or pragmatism, in a more neutral attire—and *Machtpolitik* represent the 'triangle of death' of public policy, the lines along which flows the path to extreme decisions. But hard choices can be made more easily if the outcomes are sufficiently far away not to be seen, and if they do not directly affect the government making the decision, or some higher authority that renders the choice 'right'. A bomber pilot or artillery gun crew, for instance, is likely to have less compunction about killing many individuals at the push of a button than a soldier who confronts the enemy face-to-face. Similarly, social and emotional distancing from those who bear the consequence of a life-and-death political choice follows an equivalent pattern. Sometimes it happens for pure 'pragmatic' reasons (as in the case of the Hiroshima and Nagasaki bombings), in other cases dehumanization of the enemy is the outcome of an ideology or creed: 'Opponents are always first dehumanized into hostile spectres before they are physically exterminated'.[40]

This explains how heinous conduct and atrocities are often planned by, and assigned to, those who display pathological fanaticism, severe disorders, or both:

> [C]oncentration camps were staffed, whenever possible, with 'both male and female thugs and sadists'. Unlike the victims of aerial bombing, the victims of these camps had to look their sadistic killers in the face and know that another human being denied their humanity and hated them enough to personally slaughter them, their families, and their race as though they were nothing more than animals. During strategic bombing the pilots and bombardiers were protected by distance and could deny to themselves that they were attempting to kill any specific individual.[41]

Dehumanization as a rationale to support or develop a policy, though, is not peculiar to WWII Germany. It is an essential part of standard military training to overcome the idea that an enemy is a fellow human being and to eliminate the anxiety of having to kill him; but it represents the core of the use of 'science' as a rationale for the adoption of a policy.

---

39 Ibid.
40 Habermas 1985: 185.
41 Grossman 2014: 78.

28 *Science and power*

Public policy and science

To avoid adopting public policy in the style of Callicles in *Gorgias* and resorting to manipulating the masses, the evidence upon which policies are based must have a 'scientific' value. A clear understanding of 'science' is necessary to identify which form of knowledge should shape political choices, especially in respect of national security that involves the suspension of fundamental rights.

This is not, however, a simple matter. Relying upon 'science' to justify public policy raises at least five sorts of problems that are enumerated below. But it is important to recognize that not everything that is called 'science' is actually scientific: science provides temporary explanations, not 'truth'. Being a good scientist does not mean being able to see through the lens of political and policy needs; a political decision may diverge from scientific advice because of a calculated choice or out of ignorance, scientific advice can be built 'on demand'.

Is all knowledge scientific?

There is a multitude of disciplines and experts who, qualifying themselves as 'bearers of knowledge', are candidates to be part of the decision-making authority. It is of the utmost importance that policymakers have the ability to discern which and how they can be useful to the decision-making process. Therefore, the first crucial, controversial question must be addressed: who is a 'scientist' and what exactly is 'scientific'? Does all knowledge generated by disciplines other than those traditionally associated with the world of the hard sciences qualify as 'scientific'?

Of course, it does not follow that knowledge or evidence provided by disciplines other than those conventionally regarded as pure science ought to be disregarded.

It may still be useful to policymakers. Nevertheless, social sciences seek respect as genuine sciences, and, in their pursuit for recognition, they risk being trapped in the contradiction of wanting to be 'objective' and also having a role in the decision-making process which is by nature a political or partisan process. As will be explained below, even this distinction is questionable because the role of a scientist is different from that of an adviser: the former provides 'raw data', the latter the 'interpretation' of the data or information supplied. These roles can be assigned to the very same individual, provided that they remember which side they are on when faced with a political question. In other words, when a policymaker asks, the expert should answer, 'Do you ask me as scientist or political adviser?'

Social science has played an essential part in the regulating of security issues. In the last century, to take only recent history, there has not been a single conflict that ignored the importance of economic assessments, psychological or anthropological analysis. This is true of both World Wars, the Korean war, the Vietnam war, the French Indochina war, and the Gulf and

Iraqi wars. Ruth Benedict's *The Chrysanthemum and the Sword*[42] remains an example of how relevant, not only for the good, social science has been in the context of war and security. The work is the result of research conducted during WWII on behalf of the US Office of War Information that needed to understand, and then, predict, the behaviour of Japan and the Japanese in the conduct of war. This book attracted (mostly rightly) harsh criticism which questioned its academic value[43] because of its author's lack of direct knowledge of the Japanese language and culture. Still it provides conclusive evidence of the confidence US military policymakers placed in a study by a social anthropologist and the risks of unquestioning faith in 'scientists'.

Is it merely 'the method' that turns knowledge into science?

Having long abandoned Popperian falsifiability as the only valid scientific criterion, epistemology has focused instead on the role of the intersubjective verifiability of predicates as a measure of the value of a theory:[44]

> There seems to be little awareness of the method that for several centuries has produced scientific results that everybody can acknowledge: the method based on the dissemination of the data obtained and the transparency of observational-experimental procedures that should allow repeatable results (found at different times but by the same researcher using the same techniques in the same laboratory) and reproducible (found at different times by anyone who can do so using different techniques and laboratories). Without transparency of data, empirical procedures and without reproducibility there is simply no longer the Galilean science to which we have been accustomed for several centuries: a rather obvious point, but also rather neglected, as many people warn.[45]

The different levels and combinations of data transparency and results reproducibility place the finding of a given discipline on different points along the spectrum between rigorous and heuristic value:

> If we abandon the usual methodological criteria of scientificity, how can we oppose the irrationalism we are witnessing? What difference between science and magic, between, for example, scientifically validated medical treatments and esoteric treatments proposed by charlatans and swindlers?[46]

In other words, the answer to the age-old question about social 'sciences' being qualified as such, lies not in the (self) attached label, but rather in the

---

42 Benedict 1946.
43 Watsuji 1949.
44 Dalla Pozza 2008.
45 Boniolo 2018.
46 Ibid.

30 *Science and power*

level of intersubjective verifiability of their predicates.[47] Heuristically, even though sociology, law, economics, and psychology can produce results that are of limited value or that create short-term results, they are no less important. What matters from the policymaker's point of view is the ability to identify the correct scope of the discipline that grounds its decisions, and to avoid giving general and generalizing value to theories and data that do not.

Explanation versus 'truth'

Although, as pointed out, epistemology has relinquished a deterministic view of reality for at least two centuries, its approach is still a relevant element of social 'sciences' including economics and psychology that are often an essential part of the policymaking process. While it is true that determinism is flanked by stochastic models, non-deterministic dynamic programming,[48] and other approaches disregarding a rigid causality principle, the unspoken promise of these disciplines is to foretell the future of an individual, a country, or the whole world. This is a promise that gained a new appeal from the research funded by the tech giants of the Internet-based, data driven-economy and the proliferation of neuroscience(s).[49]

With varying success, several social sciences have been applied to war and security policing. Among them, economics has gained and maintained a role of pre-eminence by virtue of the importance accorded to the adoption of a 'scientific' method: 'If the natural scientists were the model for the newly emerging social sciences, economics quickly came to be seen as the most successful adopter of that model'.[50] However the more the focus has been on the pursuit of the 'scientific' label, i.e., the growing inclusion of mathematics into research methodology, the more it has become disconnected from its utility. This phenomenon Desch calls 'the relevance problem' that reflects social scientists' contradictory desire to preserve 'objectivity' and, at the same time, to serve as support to policymakers.

Are social sciences 'objective'?

If a social science like economics is by far the most 'scientific', then studying its 'objectivity' allows one to extend its conclusions also to the other disciplines that resort less to mathematics. A 'hard' science such as economics was originally built on the pretended existence of *homo economicus*. Like *Star Trek*'s super logical Mr Spock, *homo economicus* is supposed to act

---

47 While the term 'social science' implies that disciplines such as psychology, sociology, economics are indeed 'scientific', the discussion below questions this very assumption.

48 Kira 2009.

49 Monti & Wacks 2019: 57.

50 Desch 2019: 17–18.

Science and power   31

out of sheer rationality in pursuit of his goals. In this case, though, 'hard' is not used to move economics into the domain of actual sciences such as physics or chemistry. Rather, the word is used to connote the nature of a discipline that disregards humanity and disguises its foundation, egoism, behind a facade of logic and rationality. Self-interest has nothing to do with rational calculus, and much to do with violence and greed.

Since the classical and neo-classical periods of economics, scholars were conscious of the fictional nature and (very) limited explanatory power of *homo economicus*. They therefore turned eventually to other disciplines—to psychology, in particular—and began to incorporate this 'science' into their obscure equations, hoping to acquire the 'predictive power' that had hitherto eluded them.[51] 'Behavioural economics' in its various epiphenomena (including nudge and other theories that we consider briefly below) is the attempt to overcome the limits of theories based on assumptions that contradict a 'scientific' analysis of human behaviour.

Lost in this academic wrangle, however, is the fact that neither economics nor psychology rank sufficiently high in the Parthenon of intersubjective verification of openly acquired data models previously described. Still, 'science-mantling' is a way to endow them with the appearance of a hard-science, as the words of Nobel laureate, Friedrich von Hayek recalls:

> There is as much reason to be apprehensive about the long run dangers created in a much wider field by the uncritical acceptance of assertions which have the appearance of being scientific as there is with regard to the problems I have just discussed. What I mainly wanted to bring out by the topical illustration is that certainly in my field, but I believe also generally in the sciences of man, what looks superficially like the most scientific procedure is often the most unscientific, and, beyond this, that in these fields there are definite limits to what we can expect science to achieve.[52]

This is not to say that 'science is always right' and that other disciplines are not. Science does, of course, err, but its method guarantees that errors can be detected and corrected. Moreover, science can report the extent of its findings; it uses conditional more than the indicative verbs, and is never 'right'—because scientific theories evolve and change according to the results that the research delivers:

> In the nineteenth century they use to say that Isaac Newton was one of the most intelligent men in the whole of mankind and the luckiest: there is a sole and only set of nature's fundamental laws and he himself, Isaac

---

51 Shaw 2017.
52 von Hayek 1974.

32 *Science and power*

Newton, is the lucky person who found it. Nowadays, this idea makes people smile and exposes a serious epistemological mistake made in the nineteenth century: the idea that good scientific theories are *definitive* and stay valid forever.[53]

By contrast, the findings of social sciences with the pretension of scientificity depend heavily on the hypotheses of the researcher and, as much as a scientific approach is applied, can hardly be validated. And this is the rub. Attempting to apply the scientific method is commendable, but that neither turns a discipline into a science nor gives its finding 'scientific value'. Harnessing the 'scientific method' to unreliable data does not confer explanatory power on the outcome. Otherwise astrology or parapsychology would have the right to be considered as 'scientific' simply on the ground that they process information in a 'rigorous' way.

The academic debate dating back to the WWII era is revealing of this attitude among social scientists:

> Sociologist Leslie White captured the ethos well: 'We may thus gauge the "scientific-ness" of a study by observing the extent to which it employs mathematics—the more mathematics the more scientific the study. Physics is the most mature of the sciences, and it is also the most mathematical. Sociology is the least mature of the sciences and uses very little mathematics. To make sociology scientific, therefore, we should make it mathematical … If the natural scientists were the model for the newly emerging social sciences, economics quickly came to be seen as the most successful adopter of that model'.[54]

But if data, and not only the method, make the difference, then the value of knowledge is determined by the combined effect of the former and the latter. Thus, the point is no longer to claim that discipline X is as scientific as discipline Y: each carries a certain degree of explanatory power valid within a specific context. In other words, economics or sociology can wear their 'scientific' laurels, but with the consciousness that their findings have a diminished claim to intersubjective verification.

Leaving aside semantic hair-splitting, the role of science in decision-making has been clearly identified, with ruthless pragmatism, in the field of military operations: it either provides (reliable) prediction or it is useless:

> Each war does present itself as a unique case, demanding the comprehension of its particular logic, its uniqueness. That is why the character of a war that Russia or its allies might be drawn into is very hard to

53 Rovelli 2014: 125.
54 Desch 2019: 24.

predict. Nonetheless, we must. Any academic pronouncements in military science are worthless if military theory is not backed by the function of prediction.[55]

Neutrality versus reality

If we really wish to give the term 'science' central importance, it is still possible to use it in a looser way, closer to the origin of the Latin word *scientia* that, of course, means 'knowledge'.[56] Still, adopting this linguistic route should not obliterate the difference between the effectiveness of different branches of human knowledge, for the consequences could be dramatic. This difference, clear enough in theory, is neither communicated nor understood at the political, media, or public level. The result is that political decisions and public policy may be influenced by, if not dubious, at least non-scientific outcomes which are not exposed as such by those who question the actual value of the discipline they practise.

Once again, it is important to emphasize that science is not the only form of knowledge deserving of consideration when making political choices. There might be fields of the public policy activity where science is not required at all, and where other disciplines warrant attention, as in the case of a pandemic where medicine, rather than 'science', takes the lead. Yet, as much as counterintuitive as this may seem:

> Medicine is not a science, it is a practice based on science and operating in a world of values. It is, in other words, a technique—in the Hippocratic sense of techne—endowed with its own knowledge, cognitive and evaluative, and which differs from other techniques because its object is a subject: a human being.[57]

From a public policy perspective two matters are of paramount importance: a clear understanding of the perimeters of the application of the information used to undertake a decision, and the same clear understanding of the political consequence of the given advice, whether it emanates from science or another discipline. 'Advice', though, means knowledge put into action to help achieve a result. In other words, advice is not, and cannot be neutral, as it is meant to support a political choice and not merely to provide 'rough data'. The difference between 'giving advice' and 'providing rough data' is precisely the difference between a partisan supporter of a leader, on the one hand, and a politically agnostic scientist living in his world of equations

55 Gerasimov 2013.
56 For a succinct analysis of the different meanings of the word 'science' in the modern epistemological debate, see Vissani 2019.
57 Cosmacini 2000: 11.

34   *Science and power*

and graphs, on the other. This difference, not unknown in the scientific community,[58] also characterized the evolution of social science:

> From the beginning of the twentieth century, there has been a tension between the two objectives of the evolving research university system. Science and practical application were in tension generally, but the social sciences experienced it particularly acutely. Part of this had to do with social science's more tenuous claim to being a 'science' and part of it had to do with the more political, and hence contested, focus of much social science research. This tension between these twin objectives would lead to what political scientist David Ricci termed the 'tragedy of political science': as the discipline sought to become more scientific, in part to better address society's ills, it became less practically relevant.[59]

Because of its nature, public policy abhors a vacuum created by doubt, and it is of no surprise therefore that a politician eager for a yes/no answer, or one that is required to manage unmanageable complexity, might be more at ease with 'sciences' that promise rock-solid results based on (often unspoken) deterministic approaches. In the oversimplification of the 'state-it-in-one-line' attitude of policymakers, 'science' is neutral and it is supposed to provide the magic spell that solves every problem. Science might be neutral, scientists, or, rather, 'experts', are not.

Even limiting the analysis to the security field, the COVID-19 pandemic offers many examples of the difficulty of combining decision-making power with scientific rationality. This is because deploying science to support a policy—a security policy, in particular—is a multifaceted matter and a non-linear process given the involvement of individuals with personal ambitions: politicians, various stakeholders, lobbyists, and the like. When a scientist or, say, an economist, departs his or her academic office or laboratory and provides advice or opinion they forfeit their academic or independent status, and adopt the role of political adviser. This emerges from the perceptive and prescient remarks of Nobel Laureate, Andrei Sakharov:

> There is a great deal to suggest that mankind, at the threshold of the second half of the twentieth century, entered a particularly decisive and critical period of its history.
>
> ... We cannot reject the idea of a more and more widespread use of the results of medical research or the extension of research in all its branches, including bacteriology and virology, neuro-physiology, human genetics, and gene surgery, no matter what potential dangers

---

58 Proctor 1993; Lacey 2004; Kincaid & Dupré 2007.
59 Desch 2019: 25.

lurk in their abuse and the undesirable social consequences of this research. This also applies to research which aims at creating systems for imitating intellectual processes and research involving the control of mass human behaviorism, the setting up of a unified global system of communication, systems for selecting and storing of information, and so forth. It is quite clear that in the hands of irresponsible, bureaucratic authorities operating under cover of secretiveness, all this research may prove exceptionally dangerous, but at the same time it may prove extremely important and necessary to mankind, if it is carried out under state control, testing, and socio-scientific analysis.[60]

His message is a personal one; the great Russian physicist here expresses his private opinion which has no necessary relation to his expertise or knowledge of his country's nuclear secrets.

A rational approach to public policy is of course much sought after, and countless researchers attempt to design a model to produce effective policies in the many fields of public administration.[61] Although they may be sound in theory, figures and science-based management actually translate into mantras of a new 'policy cult' whose services are officiated from the altar of 'science' by 'priests' of various kinds. Sometimes Cassandra, sometimes Rasputin, sometimes Lysenko, their role is to provide solutions to politicians' problems or 'truth-on-demand'. This does not mean that an adviser necessarily becomes a hired gun. In the interactions between adviser and policymaker, it is political acumen that makes the difference and swings the pendulum of influence toward the former or the latter.

Shades of power

There are cases, such as the United Kingdom's National DNA database, where a neutral scientific finding (the use of the DNA to identify a person) might be prejudiced by its political exploitation. As we argued elsewhere:

> This is not the place to analyse the political implications of targeting specific crimes as a genetic profiling source. Suffice it to say that if, for instance, only the authors of violent crimes are to be included in the national DNA database, and such violent crimes are mainly committed by members of a certain race or social class, the statistics based on the database-supported convictions will inevitably yield information

---

60 Sakharov 1975.
61 See, for example, Meijer & Wessels 2019; Howlett & Mukherjee 2018; Coletti 2013.

36 *Science and power*

that, notwithstanding its limited value, is likely to influence lawmakers toward targeting that specific group.[62]

In other cases, such as climate change, GMOs, and nuclear versus alternative energies, politicians decide differently and deliberately from the advice they receive from 'scientists'. But there are numerous examples of decisions based upon questionable advice devoid of scientific rationale. A paradigmatic example, related to this current pandemic, is the Avigan case, the Japanese anti-influenza drug that has gained media headlines as 'effective' against COVID-19 thanks to an amateur video broadcast by a tourist on holiday in Tokyo. The 'virality' of the video has infected so many that the Italian Medicine Agency included Avigan in the COVID-19 trials because of the social network-fuelled protests, rather than on any scientific basis. This reveals the broken interaction between science, advice, and policy. The ideal model of a scientist would say, 'There is no evidence this drug could fight COVID-19'. An equally ideal adviser would say, 'Even though the drug does not work, you might test it. If you do nothing you risk severe criticism and protests, if you do the latter you waste money, endanger genuine research but you keep the public happy'. The ideal politician (if he or she exists—even in Plato's *Hyperuranium*) would take a decision favouring public order over medical research or vice-versa. In most cases, however, a decision is likely to be taken that placates public opinion without weighing the alternatives:

> What is terrifying, as in the case of *Stamina*[63] and the various anti-cancer therapies proposed in the past, is that this tsunami of incompetence is able to convince politicians and induce esteemed agencies such as AIFA or the country's institutions to approve trials not already required by the various virologists and clinicians that these drugs (including Avigan) know them well and are fighting for us. Here we are not contesting the specific drug as much as the procedure that would lead to it in a trial that, we understand, would deprive many patients of other drugs that are currently much more promising. And it is on this basis that AIFA should not be under pressure and approve a trial based on current knowledge.[64]

The Avigan story is instructive. During the health emergency people look to 'science' as if it were a pagan deity on whose altar human sacrifices are

---

62 Monti & Wacks 2019: 45.
63 *Stamina* is the name of a method invented in 2007 by Davide Vannoni, an Italian psychologist (not a medical doctor) allegedly able to cure neuro-degenerative diseases. Notwithstanding its complete lack of scientificity, and owing to the heat generated by a TV show, *Stamina* was allowed by the courts to be administered in public hospitals and later tested by the public health system with a 3 million Euro budget diverted from other testing programmes. See, among others, Abbott 2013; Margottini 2014.
64 Bucci, Corbellini, & De Luca 2020.

Science and power 37

offered. And when the miracle of a cure does not materialize the irrational reaction is to punish the divinity, putting it on trial in the name of the infringement of a supposed 'duty of salvation'.[65] Permitting public opinion rather than scientists and advisers to determine a decision is a sure way toward turning citizens into a mob of insurgents.

From another perspective, 'science' as an instrument of regulation is often perceived by policymakers as a cog in the decision-making process that works in a deterministic fashion, like all the other administrative mechanisms are supposed to do. In the rigidity of a (public) policy, all the nuances of the interactions between science, advice, and policymakers collapse into formal determinism. A single provision, a statute, for instance, at least on paper, operates as a rigid cause-effect mechanism: 'Do X and you will achieve Y'. By contrast (genuine) scientific predicates do not fit well into this decisional design. And so, together with 'scientific' theories, decision-makers need, or need as well, numbers to support their decisions—because numbers and statistics do not lie.

Statistics can lie

Among the many sciences abused during the COVID-19 pandemic, statistics is undoubtedly the one that has suffered most. Blatantly disregarding the World Health Organization's caveat[66] that clearly warns about differences in reporting methods, a confused public has been bombarded throughout the crisis by analyses and 'readings' of facts based on conceptual confusion, unreliable data, and gross errors amplified by the mainstream media and online sources. The United Kingdom government adopted a five-pillar strategy[67] where the first stage is swab-testing. The spreading of the virus is measured by mass swab-testing of the population with symptoms while

---

65 Finally overruled by the Italian Supreme Court, a first degree decision indicted scientists members of the governmental High Risk Commission tasked in the aftermath of the earthquake of 6 April 2009 that struck the Abruzzo Region. The scientists were tried for not having foreseen what was unpredictable: the occurrence of the earthquake. While *excusatio non petita*, the judge of first instance had to specify that he did not intend to put science on trial, but it is also true that the defendants were accused of carrying out a 'risk assessment of the seismic activity in progress on the territory of L'Aquila since December 2008 approximate, generic and ineffective in relation to the activities and duties of prediction and prevention'. The accusation is fundamentally contradictory: either earthquakes can be predicted, and then the 'assessment of the risks involved' is possible, or they are not. If the latter, not only can there be no 'risk assessment' but neither can there be a duty to predict and prevent the event.

66 World Health Organization 'Coronavirus disease 2019 (COVID-19) Situation Report—87'. www.who.int/docs/default-source/coronaviruse/situation-reports/20200416-sitrep-87-covid-19.pdf?sfvrsn=9523115a_2 (Visited 20 April 2020).

67 Coronavirus (COVID-19): scaling up our testing programmes. www.gov.uk/government/publications/coronavirus-covid-19-scaling-up-testing-programmes/coronavirus-covid-19-scaling-up-our-testing-programmes (Visited 20 April 2020).

38   *Science and power*

excluding the results of anti-body testing.[68] Moreover, the National Health Service counts deaths by COVID-19 whoever dies 'with' rather than 'from' the virus.[69]

In Italy, the first country to have suffered a considerable number of infections, the Ministry of Health adopted a British-like approach by providing figures rather than statistics,[70] but the National Civil Protection, a department of the Prime Minister's Office, quietly misinterpreted the significance of statistics in its official statements. A press release accounting for the infection-spreading claims stated, 'For the first time, the number of positives is decreasing',[71] but, as will be argued below, this statement is meaningless without the inclusion of a reference point.

The Spanish government included percentages in its reports and provided an official 'lethality rate' based on the ratio between confirmed cases only (thus not counting the infected 'dark number') and deaths.[72] France limited the testing to serious cases only, meaning that

> it does not count the exact number of infected people, which is much higher. The difference between the number of cases actually infected and those counted is therefore much greater in France than in Germany. This mathematically increases the French mortality rate, which is calculated by reducing the number of deaths to the total number of registered cases.[73]

Germany, on the other hand, chose a stricter criterion to qualify a person as COVID-19 positive, and conducted a considerably more comprehensive testing programme. It would seem that this explains its early success in containing the spread of the virus. Epidemiological confirmation, according to the Robert Koch Institute, is defined

---

68 'The UK total is not the sum of the four nations' totals as the pillar 2 cases cannot currently be included in the nations' totals. All other data on this website are based only on cases detected through pillar 1'—Coronavirus (COVID-19) cases in the UK. https://coronavirus.data.gov.uk/about (Visited 20 April 2020).

69 Coronavirus (COVID-19) cases in the UK. https://coronavirus.data.gov.uk/about (Visited 20 April 2020).

70 COVID-19—Situazione in Italia. www.salute.gov.it/imgs/C_17_notizie_4539_0_file.pdf

71 Dipartimento della protezione civile—Comunicato stampa 'Coronavirus: la situazione dei contagi in Italia'—April 20, 2020. www.protezionecivile.gov.it/media-comunicazione/co municati-stampa/dettaglio/-/asset_publisher/default/content/coronavirus-la-situazione-dei-contagi-in-ital-2 (Visited 20 April 2020).

72 Ministerio de Sanidad—Centro de Coordinación de Alertas y Emergencias Sanitarias—Actualización n° 60. Enfermedad por el coronavirus (COVID-19) 31 March 2020. www.m scbs.gob.es/en/profesionales/saludPublica/ccayes/alertasActual/nCov-China/documentos/Actualizacion_61_COVID-19.pdf (Visited 20 April 2020).

73 Goupil 2020.

as at least one of the following two types of evidence, taking into account the incubation period:

- epidemiological link with a laboratory diagnostic proven infection in humans through human-to-human transmission
- occurrence of two or more pneumoniae (specific clinical picture) in a medical facility, nursing or old people's home, where an epidemic link is probable or suspected, even without the presence of a pathogen detection incubation period maximum 14 days.[74]

In the United States, the definition of a 'COVID-19 case' includes confirmed and probable cases. It defines such cases by reference to five criteria ranging from clinical observation (specific symptoms with no alternative diagnosis), to laboratory analysis (antibody or antigen detection, presence of COVID-19 genetic traces), from epidemiologic linkage (symptoms plus interaction with potentially contagious places or persons) to *post-mortem* certificates stating that COVID-19 is the cause of death or a significant contribution to death and, finally, to autopsies detecting 'pneumonia or acute respiratory distress syndrome without an identifiable cause'.[75] A 'probable case' is defined as follows:

- Meeting clinical criteria AND epidemiologic evidence with no confirmatory laboratory testing performed for COVID-19; or
- Meeting presumptive laboratory evidence AND either clinical criteria OR epidemiologic evidence; or
- Meeting vital records criteria with no confirmatory laboratory testing performed for COVID-19.[76]

Between 15 January and 3 March 2020 China adopted seven different versions of a criteria-set to define a COVID-19 case:

From Jan 15 to March 3, 2020, seven versions of the case definition for COVID-19 were issued by the National Health Commission in China. We estimated that when the case definitions were changed, the

---

74 Robert Koch Institute 'Falldefinition Coronavirus Disease 2019 (COVID-19) (SARS-CoV-2), Stand March 24, 2020'. www.rki.de/DE/Content/InfAZ/N/Neuartiges_Coronavir us/Falldefinition.pdf;jsessionid=85265CF5E794AE445BCBC24AC1634FA3.internet0 72?__blob=publicationFile (Visited 20 April 2020).

75 US Council of State and Territorial Epidemiologists 'Standardized surveillance case definition and national notification for 2019 novel coronavirus disease (COVID-19)' 5 April 2020. https://cdn.ymaws.com/www.cste.org/resource/resmgr/2020ps/Interim-20-ID-01_COVID-19.pdf (Visited 3 May 2020).

76 US Center for Disease Control and Prevention 'FAQ: COVID-19 Data and Surveillance: What is a COVID-19 case?' 17 April 2020. www.cdc.gov/coronavirus/2019-ncov/covid-data/faq-surveillance.html (Visited 4 May 2020).

40 *Science and power*

proportion of infections being detected as cases increased by 7·1 times (95% credible interval [CrI] 4·8–10·9) from version 1 to 2, 2·8 times (1·9–4·2) from version 2 to 4, and 4·2 times (2·6–7·3) from version 4 to 5. If the fifth version of the case definition had been applied throughout the outbreak with sufficient testing capacity, we estimated that by Feb 20, 2020, there would have been 232 000 (95% CrI 161 000–359 000) confirmed cases in China as opposed to the 55 508 confirmed cases reported.[77]

South Korea adopted a different policy: a massive testing of the population at the first arrival of the virus in the country. This facilitated the early detection of actual cases, producing more reliable figures without waiting for patients to be hospitalized.[78]

These few examples demonstrate the importance of a standard (and reliable) definition of what constitutes a COVID-19 (probable) case and (probable) death from the disease to support decision-makers' adoption of a specific policy in the security and safety domain. Without clear principles upon which the counting of COVID-19 cases is based, the resulting policy choices become problematic. Should we swab? Do we include first-aid reports? Do we exclude asymptomatic individuals? Is the same type of swab kit being used by those administering the test? Do they all follow the same protocol? How reliable is the swab or blood tests? And so on. Similar reasoning applies to the counting of deaths, including a distinction drawn between patients who die 'with' as opposed to 'from' the virus. Some deaths occur as a direct result of COVID-19; others have co-morbidities. Still others die because, even though they have not contracted the infection, they cannot be treated in time because of the overcrowding in hospitals. Their deaths may be caused by cardiac arrest, stroke, or anaphylactic shock. These distinctions may be irrelevant if it is intended to assess the overall impact of the pandemic but is indispensable for strictly medical-scientific assessments of lethality and mortality rates:

The UK has mainly tested people who are ill enough to be admitted to hospital. That can make the death rate appear much higher than in a country which had a wider testing programme. The more testing a

---

77 Tsang et al. (2020).
78 South Korean Central Disaster and Safety Countermeasure Headquarters 'Current Status of Response to COVID-19 and Future Plans' 9 March 2020. http://ncov.mohw.go.kr/board/doFileDownload.do?file_name=200309%20Current%20Status%20of%20Response%20to%20COVID-19%20and%20Future%20Plans.pdf&file_path=/upload/ncov/file/202004/1588144040684_20200429160720.pdf&seq=3843 (Visited 8 May 2020).

Science and power 41

country carries out, the more it will find people who have coronavirus with only mild symptoms, or perhaps no symptoms at all.

So, the death rate in confirmed cases is not the same as the overall death rate.[79]

The same fate affects lethality and mortality rates that are 'influenced' by the definition of 'COVID-19 deaths'. In the UK these are considered to be those of every patient who tested positive or is even suspected of being infected regardless of the actual cause of death.[80] Germany and Hong Kong include in the list both the patients who died 'with' COVID-19 and 'from' COVID-19.

The result of these disparities in criteria is that at a national level the figures have very limited statistical value; that the number of cases in Country A cannot meaningfully be compared with the number in Country B. It is hard to make sense out of data whose origin differs from country to country and at different times within a single country. But even more complications occur when data are presented in graphic form.[81]

Calculating the number of COVID-19 positive individuals (let alone the questions pertaining to differences in definition) is a matter of tallying the daily figures from national health services, not from a statistical sample. So, for example, suppose on Monday a hospital reports 10 infected patients; on Tuesday it reports 39; on Wednesday, 23 and counting. All these data, once transformed into a chart, acquire a powerful explanatory capability as the audience perceive the visual impact without connecting it to the underlying figures.[82] A histogram showing 5 infected today and 15 infected tomorrow produces on the second day a bar three times higher than the previous one. Strictly speaking, the visual ratio is correct but the information depicted or suggested by the chart (a huge increase in the rate of infection) is not.

Another critical misperception of the analysis of the evolution of COVID-19 is to believe that the 'curve' of contagion is the result of a 'formula' (like the famous $y = ax^2 + bx + c$ that populated the nightmares of teenagers' tetragons of analytical geometry) when instead it is based on periodic data collection. The difference is significant because in the first case the curve is 'predictive' in the sense that it allows the calculation of the values of the coordinates at any point of the curve itself. In the second case, however, the curve is a 'snapshot', i.e., it provides 'instantaneous values' but without the past and the present being allowed to say something about the future in regard to the evolution of the pandemic. By contrast, such data are useful to track the response to the system (where to test more, how to improve

79 Morris & Reuben 2020.
80 Enriques 2020.
81 Huff 1954.
82 Chiqui 2015.

42 *Science and power*

the number of swabs, how to back-trace infected individuals' movements, etc.) but this is not the way they are communicated by governments and the media or how they are interpreted by the public.

Numbers as an instrument of social control

In general, official sources have been careful to report only the absolute numbers affected by the contagion and not to convert them into percentages. They have also been scrupulous in pointing out when the number of infected individuals was derived from the results of swab tests carried out and therefore placing citizens in the (formal) position to be able to understand that this information is not statistically valid.

It is not entirely surprising that the often sensationalist coverage by the media of the spread of the pandemic has induced panic and anxiety.[83] This has facilitated the acceptance of Draconian measures, such as the limitation or suspension of constitutional rights, as well as an increased willingness by the public to tolerate police checks.[84] In the UK there is even the suggestion that by their emotive coverage of the contagion, certain elements of the media have infantilized the public, already generated by the ubiquitous presence of smartphones and electronic devices.[85]

[T]he infantilist ethos becomes especially seductive in times of social crises and fear. And its favoring of simple, easy and fast betrays natural affinities for certain political solutions over others. And typically not intelligent ones.

Democratic policymaking requires debate, demands compromise and involves critical thinking. It entails considering different viewpoints, anticipating the future, and composing thoughtful legislation.

What's a fast, easy and simple alternative to this political process? It's not difficult to imagine an infantile society being attracted to authoritarian rule.

Unfortunately, our social institutions and technological devices seem to erode hallmarks of maturity: patience, empathy, solidarity, humility and commitment to a project greater than oneself.

All are qualities that have traditionally been considered essential for both healthy adulthood and for the proper functioning of democracy.[86]

The most obvious manifestation of the interaction between the 'acquired logical resignation', 'technologically induced infantilization', and public

---

83 Seligman 1972.
84 Seligman 2011. See Chapter 5.
85 Goodhart 2020.
86 Gottschalk 2018.

Science and power 43

policy is represented by the debate on contact tracing that fizzled around the European Union.

We have known for centuries that 'social distancing' and the detection of infected individuals are the key measures deployed to stem the spread of a virus. Their modern iteration is little more than a more homely application of quarantine, and the age-old hunt for plague-spreaders described, for example, in the *Storia della colonna infame*[87] and the massacres in Barcelona and La Baume.[88]

Our concern should not therefore be concentrated upon the feasibility of social distancing and the identification of the infected—quarantine and hunting of the plague-spreaders—but on the manner in which these measures are implemented through mass control technology that, in recent years, has reached alarmingly invasive capacity. The question thus becomes to decide where we stand in our choice between two extremes. On the one hand, there is State-imposed technological control and a 'manhunt'; on the other hand, there is blind faith in the human ability to 'do the right thing' morally. It is a matter, in other words, of reconciling the extent of individual control, the efficacy of public security and safety measures, and individual and collective rights. Balancing the public interest and individual rights is precisely what one would hope our governments exercise with prudence and care, but this longstanding expectation remains a precarious one.

References

Abbott, Alison. 2013. 'Italian Stem-Cell Trial Based on Flawed Data', *Nature*, online edition, 2 July. www.nature.com/news/italian-stem-cell-trial-based-on-fl awed-data-1.13329 (Visited 26 April 2020).

Badoglio, Pietro. 1946. *L'Italia nella seconda guerra mondiale (Memorie e documenti)*. Milan: Arnoldo Mondadori Editore.

Barnes, David M. 2016. *The Ethics of Military Privatization (Military and Defence Ethics)*. Abingdon: Taylor and Francis.

Benedict, Ruth. 1946. *The Chrysanthemum and the Sword: Patterns of Japanese Culture*. Boston, MA: Houghton Miffin.

Bernays, Edward. 1928. *Propaganda*. New York: Horace Liveright.

Black, Edwin. 2001. *IBM and the Holocaust: Strategic Alliance between Nazi Germany and America's Most Powerful Corporation*. New York: Crown Books.

Boniolo, Giovanni. 2018. Più etica, metodologia e filosofia per lo scienziato in Scienza in rete. 22 December. www.scienzainrete.it/articolo/pi%C3%B9-etica-metodologia-e-filosofia-lo-scienziato/giovanni-boniolo/2018-12-12 (Visited 24 April 2020).

Bucci, Enrico, Gilberto Corbellini and Michele De Luca. 2020. 'AVIGAN e le terapie a furor di popolo', *Science*, 28 March. www.scienzainrete.it/articolo/avigan-e-l

---

87 Manzoni 1840.
88 Ginzburg 2017: 41–61.

44   *Science and power*

e-terapie-furor-di-popolo/enrico-bucci-gilberto-corbellini-michele-de-luca/2020 (Visited 20 April 2020).

Chiqui, Esteban. 2015. 'A Quick Guide to Spotting Graphics That Lie', *National Geographic*, 19 June. www.nationalgeographic.com/news/2015/06/150619-dat a-points-five-ways-to-lie-with-charts/ (Visited 9 May 2020).

Chomsky, Noam. 1989. *Manufacturing Consent*. Boston, MA: South End Press.

Coletti, Paola. 2013. *Evidence for Public Policy Design: How to Learn from Best Practice*. London: Palgrave Macmillan.

Cosmacini, Giorgio. 2000. *Il mestiere di medico*. Milan: Raffaello Cortina Editore.

Dalla Pozza, Carlo. 2008. *Il problema della demarcazione. Verificabilità, falsificabilità e confermabilità bayesana a confronto*. Lecce: Editoria Scientifica Elettronica Università del Salento.

Del Guercio, Gino. 1986. 'The Secrets of Haiti's Living Dead', *Harvard Review*, January-February. www.harvardmagazine.com/2017/10/are-zombies-real (Visited 13 May 2020).

Desch, Michael. 2019. *Cult of the Irrelevant. (Princeton Studies in International History and Politics)*. Princeton, NJ: Princeton University Press.

Enriques, Martha. 2020. 'Coronavirus: Why Death and Mortality Rates Differ?', *BBC Future*, 2 April. www.bbc.com/future/article/20200401-coronavirus-wh y-death-and-mortality-rates-differ (Visited 25 April 2020).

Foucault, François de La Roche. 1749. Moral Maxims by the Duke de La Roche Foucault, translated from the French, with notes. London: A Millar.

Gerasimov, Valery. 2013. 'The Value of Science Is in the Foresight: New Challenges Demand Rethinking the Forms and Methods of Carrying out Combat Operations', trans. Robert Coalson, Military Industrial Kurier, 27 February in *Military Review*. January-February 2016 edition. www.armyupress.army.mil/P ortals/7/military-review/Archives/English/MilitaryReview:20160228_art008.pdf (Visited 30 April 2020).

Ginzburg, Carlo. 2017. *Storia Notturna. Una decifrazione del sabba*. Palermo: Adelphi, English edition, 2004, Ecstasies: Deciphering the Witches' Sabbath. Chicago, IL: Chicago University Press.

Goodhart, David. 2020. 'Pass the Remote, There's Too Much Emotion on the News', *Sunday Times*, 26 April. www.thetimes.co.uk/article/dcb2fb4a-86d0 -11ea-8883-462ecf1d0616?shareToken=6b13cfcb14fd2d6254117d24fbc931c8 (Visited 27 April 2020).

Gottschalk, Simon. 2018. 'The Infantilization of Western Culture', *The Conversation*, 1 August. https://theconversation.com/the-infantilization-of-western-culture-995 56 (Visited 26 April 2020).

Goupil, Mathilde. 2020. 'Coronavirus : pourquoi le taux de mortalité est-il aussi faible en Allemagne?', *France Info*, online edition, 18 March. www.francetvinf o.fr/sante/maladie/coronavirus/coronavirus-pourquoi-le-taux-de-mortalite-est-il-aussi-faible-en-allemagne_3871743.html (Visited 20 April 2020).

Grossman, Dave. 2014 *On Killing: The Psychological Cost of Learning to Kill in War and Society*. New York: Open Road Media.

Habermas, Jürgen. 1985. *Observations on The Spiritual Situation of the Age: Contemporary German Perspectives (Studies in Contemporary German Social Thought)*. Cambridge, MA: MIT Press.

Hasegawa, Tsuyoshi. 2005. *Racing The Enemy: Stalin, Truman, And The Surrender of Japan*. Cambridge, MA: Belknap Press.

Science and power   45

Hazan, Barukh. 2017. *Soviet Propaganda: A Case Study of the Middle East Conflict.* Abingdon: Routledge.

Hisho, Saito. 1912. *A History of Japan.* Abingdon: Routledge.

Howlett, Michael and Ishani Mukherjee. 2018. *Routledge Handbook of Policy Design.* Abingdon: Routledge.

Huff, Darrell. 1954. *How to Lie with Statistics.* New York: Norton & Co.

Kincaid, Harold and John Dupré. 2007. *Value-Free Science? Ideals and Illusion.* New York: Oxford University Press.

Kira, Akifumi and Fujita, Toshiharu. 2009. 'Double versus triple competitive processes: non-deterministic model' Mathematical Sciences, Kyoto University, Vol.1654/2009, pp. 19–34. www.kurims.kyoto-u.ac.jp/~kyodo/kokyuroku/contents/pdf/1654-02.pdf (Visited 22 April 2020.

Krige, John. 2014. 'Technological Collaboration and Nuclear Proliferation: A Transnational Approach', in Mayer, Maximilian, Carpes, Mariana and Knoblich, Ruth (eds.), *The Global Politics of Science and Technology.* Berlin: Springer.

Lacey, Hugh. 2004. *Is Science Value Free? Values and Scientific Understanding.* Abingdon: Routledge.

Liu, Eric. 2014. 'How to Understand Power', *Ted-Ed Talk.* https://youtu.be/c_Eutci7ack—Transcripts available at www.ted.com/talks/eric_liu_how:to_understand_power/transcript?language=en (Visited 9 April 2020).

Lowsen, Ben. 2020. 'Did Xi Jinping Deliberately Sicken the World?', *The Diplomat,* online edition, 15 April. https://thediplomat.com/2020/04/did-xi-jinping-deliberately-sicken-the-world/ (Visited 16 April 2020).

Luttwak, Edward N. 2016. *Coup d'État: A Practical Handbook,* Revised edition. Cambridge, MA: Harvard University Press.

Manzoni, Alessandro. 1840. *Storia della colonna infame.* Milan: Tipografia Guglielmini e Redaelli.

Margottini, Laura. 2014. 'Final Chapter in Italian Stem Cell Controversy?', *ScienceMag,* online edition, 7 October. www.sciencemag.org/news/2014/10/final-chapter-italian-stem-cell-controversy (Visited 26 April 2020).

Meijer, Albert and Martijn Wessels. 2019. 'Predictive Policing: Review of Benefits and Drawbacks', *International Journal of Public Administration,* 42(12): 1031–1039.

Montalto Monella, Lillo. 2020. 'Coronavirus: Italy Doctors Forced to Prioritise ICU Care for Patients with Best Chance of Survival', *Euronews,* online edition, 13 March. www.euronews.com/embed/1045632 (Visited 19 April 2020).

Monti, Andrea and Raymond Wacks. 2019. *Protecting Personal Information: The Right to Privacy Reconsidered.* Oxford: Hart Publishing.

Moran, Michael, Martin Rein and Robert E. Goodin. 2008. *The Oxford Handbook of Public Policy.* Oxford: Oxford University Press.

Morris, C. and A. Reuben. 2020. 'Coronavirus: Why Are International Comparisons Difficult?', *BBC Reality Check,* 21 April. www.bbc.com/news/52311014 (Visited 24 April 2020).

Orwell, George.1948. *Nineteen Eighty-Four.* Boston, MA: Mifflin Harcourt.

Packard, Vance. 1959. *The Hidden Persuaders.* New York: Pocket Books.

Pandurang, Vaman Kane. 1930, 1962. *History of Dharmaśāstra. Ancient and Mediaeval Religions and Civil Law in India.* Pune: Bhandarkar Oriental Research Institute.

46 Science and power

Paresky, Pamela. 2020. 'The Moral Dilemma of Coronavirus: Is it Lives Versus Money?', *Jewish Journal*, online edition, 29 March. https://jewishjournal.com/online/312925/moral-dilemma-coronavirus-money-lives/ (Visited 19 April 2020).

Proctor, Robert. 1993. Value-Free Science? Purity and Power in Modern Knowledge. Cambridge, MA: Harvard University Press.

Ravi, Agrawal. 2016. 'India's Caste System: Outlawed, but Still Omnipresent', *CNN*, online edition, 24 February. https://edition.cnn.com/2016/02/23/asia/india-caste-system/index.html (Visited 9 April 2020).

Ridgen, Denis. 2004. *How to Be a Spy: The World War II SOE Training Manual Dundurn*. Toronto: Dundurn Press.

Riesman, David. 1947, 2001. *The Lonely Crowd: A Study of the Changing American Character*, revised edition. New Haven: Yale University Press.

Rovelli, Carlo. 2014. *Cos'è la scienza? La rivoluzione di Anassimandro*. Milan: Mondadori.

Sakharov, Andrei. 1975. 'Peace, Progress, Human Rights' Nobel Lecture', 11 December. www.nobelprize.org/prizes/peace/1975/sakharov/lecture/ (русская версия www.nobelprize.org/nobel_prizes/peace/laureates/1975/sakharov-lecture-ru.html) (Visited 27 April 2020).

Seligman, Martin. 1972. 'Learned Helplessness', *Annual Review of Medicine*, 23.

Seligman, Martin. 2011. 'Risk for Fundamental Rights is Learned Helplessness', *Harvard Business Review*. https://hbr.org/2011/04/building-resilience (Visited 10 May 2020).

Shaw, Adam. 2017. 'Why Economic Forecasting Has Always Been a Flawed Science', *The Guardian*, online edition, 2 September. www.theguardian.com/money/2017/sep/02/economic-forecasting-flawed-science-data (Visited 18 April 2020).

Taylor, Philip. 1997. *Global Communications, International Affairs and the Media Since 1945*. Abingdon: Routledge.

Thaler, Richard and Sunstein, Cass. 2009. *Nudge: Improving Decisions About Health, Wealth, and Happiness*. New York: Penguin Group.

Tsang,Tim, Lin Peng, Lau Eric Yu, Gabriel Leung and Benjamin Cowling. 2020. 'Effect of Changing Case Definitions for COVID-19 on the Epidemic Curve and Transmission Parameters in Mainland China: a Modelling Study', *The Lancet*, 5(5): E289–E296 https://doi.org/10.1016/S2468-2667(20)30089-X (Visited 7 May 2020).

Vissani, Francesco. 2019. 'Benedetto Croce, la scienza e la scuola', *Quaderni di Cultura Scientifica*, 1: 17. 19 November. Available at the Gran Sasso Science Institute—www.gssi.it/people/professors/lectures-physics/item/download/2089_5db1115c7146b7fd7ce74c81168334ee (Visited 20 April 2020).

von Clausewitz, Carl. 1984. *On War*, trans. and ed. by Howard, Michael and Peter Paret. Princeton, NJ: Princeton University Press.

von Hayek, Friedrich. 1974. 'Prize Lecture'. www.nobelprize.org/prizes/economic-sciences/1974/hayek/lecture/ (Visited 16 April 2020).

Wacks, Raymond. 2020. *Understanding Jurisprudence: An Introduction to Legal Theory*, 6th ed. Oxford: Oxford University Press.

Watsuji, Tetsurō. 1949. 'Queries on the Scientific Value of *The Chrysanthemum and the Sword* in Minzokugaku Kenkyū, 14(4) English Translation by Tokita-Tanabe, Yumiko in *Japanese*', Review of Cultural Anthropology, 17(1): 2016. www.jstage.jst.go.jp/article/jrca/17/1/17_037/_pdf (Visited 30 April 2020).

Weber, Max. 1951. *The Religion of China: Confucianism and Taoism*, trans. and ed. by Hans H. Gerth. Glencoe, IL: Free Press.

Weber, Max. 1954. Max Weber on Law in Economy and Society, ed. Max Rheinstein, trans. Edward Shils and Max Rheinstein. 20th Century Legal Philosophy Series, vol 6. Cambridge, MA: Harvard University Press.

Welch, David. 1993. 'Manufacturing a Consensus: Nazi Propaganda and the Building of a "National Community" (Volksgemeinschaft)', *Contemporary European History*, 2(1): 1–15.

Young, Louise. 1998. *Japan's Total Empire. Manchuria and the Culture of Wartime Imperialism*. Berkeley, MA: University of California Press.

Young, Toby. 2020. 'Has the Government Overreacted to the Coronavirus Crisis?', *The Critic*, online edition, 31 March. https://thecritic.co.uk/has-the-governme nt-over-reacted-to-the-coronavirus-crisis/ (Visited 19 April 2020).

3 Law, rights, and public policy

> The end of the law is not to abolish or restrain but to preserve and enlarge freedom.
>
> John Locke

Emergencies present opportunities for authoritarian governments to flout the values inherent in democratic societies. COVID-19 is a test of the resilience and strength of civil liberties and the rule of law. The inevitable suspension of individual freedoms necessitated by the campaign against the pandemic nevertheless dictates that a delicate balance be struck between freedom and public health. This chapter considers the extent to which this has been achieved.

The impact on civil liberties

In principle, pre-emptive surveillance, plague-spreader identification, mandatory containment, and quarantine are appropriate means of control in a pandemic. But this inexorably requires resorting to public order and public security structures: the police and, in extreme cases, the military. From a legal standpoint inadequate attention has been paid to the extent to which the effective enforcement of such measures is inextricably linked to public security and public order regulations. While it is the disease control authorities who require these controls to be adopted, and the government which legislates them, ultimately law enforcement and judicial authorities ensure that they are effectively enforced. This gives rise to important considerations regarding the impact on individual rights and the rule of law.

The age-old tension between 'security' and 'freedom' arises whenever a State invokes the former to justify the sometimes Draconian restrictions on individual rights. In the case of the Coronavirus pandemic, however, this is a somewhat abstract debate because the legal framework of domestic and international fundamental rights has been largely unaffected by the pandemic. But the same cannot be said for governmental powers—exceptional or otherwise—whose enforcement poses

Law, rights, and public policy 49

the question whether public policy 'is more devoted to "order" than to justice'.[1]

When considering the conflict between security and freedom, it is important to recognize how much the debate has been profoundly affected by the manner in which fear has, in recent years, changed our way of life:

> We are searched for weapons before boarding a plane, visiting city hall, seeing a television show taping, or attending a speech by the president. Our government buildings are surrounded by barricades, and we wrestle through so-called tamper-proof packaging to get a couple aspirin. All of this was triggered by the deeds of fewer than ten dangerous men who got our attention by frightening us. What other quorum in American history, save those who wrote our Constitution, could claim as much impact on our day-to-day lives?[2]

We must also acknowledge that (national) security threats have been used to sponsor legislation and public policies that facilitate greater governmental control, including extended surveillance programmes and the power to deny access to the European Union to people 'responsible' for cybercrime, despite their not being charged with an offence. Nevertheless, the threats to our security such as terrorist attacks and related criminal acts have so far had only a limited impact on civil liberties:

> Whatever the intrusive and annoying nature of antiterrorist measures … it is a grotesque exaggeration to claim that our citizens' civil liberties and civil rights have been grossly compromised by these measures, especially when these practices have been subject to independent review by the judiciary in the U.S. and the U.K.[3]

Moreover, the scale of these threats remains fairly low despite the sometimes exaggerated claims in the media and elsewhere. Although affected countries speak of a 'global' war on terrorism, its 'globality' is related to the geographic and geopolitical reach of the military and covert operations rather than to the direct involvement of the population of the world as a whole. Courts have generally displayed a fairly robust defence of the rule of law against attacks launched by executive authorities, who, when violations of liberty have been exposed—mass surveillance programmes, the detention of individuals without probable cause, or extraordinary renditions in foreign countries without official sanction—have had to step back from such

---

1 Martin Luther King Jr. 1963, Martin Jr. 'Letter from a Birmingham Jail' 16 April 1963. www.africa.upenn.edu/Articles_Gen/Letter_Birmingham.html (Visited 23 May 2020).
2 De Becker 1997: 11.
3 Bobbitt 2008: 206.

50 *Law, rights, and public policy*

encroachments. This does not mean they will shrink from circumventing political and judicial checks, but the *principle* of the rule of law is widely sustained and upheld.

Of course, as the boiling frog metaphor suggests, the small but continual acceptance of the curtailment of rights can, over time, reduce them to formal, empty statements with limited practical application.

The perception of restricted civil liberties

The public perception of the spread of the pandemic played a critical role in surrendering 'special powers' to governments, and in the acceptance of their enforcement. In order to rationalize these inroads into civil liberties, a convincing justification is called for. To this end, possibly because of a Pavlovian reflex or out of a well-conceived strategy, the media and governments have not confined themselves to the use of science and relevant data, but also deployed bellicose metaphors that have played a critical role in convincing the public that warlike 'special powers' were necessary to 'defeat' the pandemic.

Self-preservation, whether triggered by an actual global danger or by an induced state of fear, has reduced the sensitivity to the importance of preserving many of the democratic achievements of Western society. The perception of the threat has coaxed individuals into relinquishing their rights, so much so that it is no hyperbole to claim that our sensitivity to the erosion of our rights has itself eroded. This is less the fault of the virus than the manner in which it has been 'communicated'. And it is not to diminish the gravity of the pandemic; quite the opposite. But while the management of an emergency on this scale required information to be collected, analyzed, and delivered with the greatest care, the response in almost every country has approached hysteria, confusion, and contradictory policies. In particular, the media's propensity for alarmism contributed to a state of uncertainty that engendered a sense of vulnerability and helplessness:

> Exacerbating the widespread stress of this crisis, many of us are suffering significant personal losses and grief reactions, which are robust predictors of depression. The ongoing and unpredictable course of these stressors adds an additional layer of risk.[4]

The universal cry of 'waging war'[5] may be apposite in the context of geopolitical propaganda about 'Cold War II' between the United States and China, but, as is discussed below, it is less advisable when confronting a pandemic. The rhetoric (doctors and health workers described as 'heroes')

---

4 Kanter & Manbeck 2020.
5 Tian 2020; De Bernardi 2020; Brady 2020.

Law, rights, and public policy 51

exploited by politicians and the media is an integral part of this militaristic metaphor, particularly in the United States:

> [A]gonism—taking a warlike stance in contexts that are not literally war—pervades our public and private discourse, leading us to approach issues and each other in an adversarial spirit. The resulting 'argument culture' makes it more difficult to solve problems and is corrosive to the human spirit ... By creating an atmosphere of animosity, it makes individuals more likely to turn on each other, so that everyone feels more vulnerable and more isolated. And that is why the argument culture is destructive to the common good.[6]

It contributed to the panic and selfishness that saw stockpiling in supermarkets across the globe. The role of metaphor in shaping Coronavirus-related public opinion and public policy cannot be overstated. Metaphor is 'a pervasive, irreducible, imaginative structure of human understanding that influences the nature of meaning and constrains our rational inferences'.[7] The intrinsic ambiguity of metaphors that led Hobbes—metaphorically—to call them *ignes fatui*[8] is precisely what makes them valuable in the psychotherapy to heal,[9] in advertising to convince,[10] and, in politics, to deceive.[11]

But, as already mentioned, we are not waging war against the virus. The psychological effects of war on civilians include post-traumatic stress disorder, depression, anxiety, and other forms of emotional distress.[12] While the COVID-19 containment measures caused similar problems; in times of war, it is relatively easy to justify the need to expose spies, and covert enemy operators require exceptional measures. The requirement to supply soldiers on the frontline warrants an acceptance of the scarcity of goods, and that in extremely harsh conditions the first rule is 'survive', sometimes overlooking social solidarity. Moreover, even in the case of an enemy invasion or occupation people maintain at least a mild awareness of their rights when challenging abusive conduct by the enemy.[13] Encountering an invisible, overwhelming, non-human threat is not a personal attack against a country or a nation. There is nobody to be united against, no place to hide, and no way to fight back:

6 Tannen 2013.
7 Johnson 1987: xii.
8 Hobbes 1651: 22.
9 Kirmayer 1988: 157–172.
10 Tanaka 1994.
11 Dittmer 1977: 552–583.
12 Hanson and Vogel 2012: 412.
13 Gargiulo 2018.

52 *Law, rights, and public policy*

> [W]hen you're in a struggle with one of Mother Nature's challenges—like a virus or a climate change—the goal is not to defeat her. No one can. She's just chemistry, biology and physics. The goal is to adapt.[14]

It is therefore evident that combative metaphors

> aren't particularly well suited for telling people what not to do. 'War metaphors call for mobilization, for action, for doing something', Veronika Koller, a linguist at Lancaster University in England, told me. In this pandemic, governments are asking people to do the opposite: to forgo normal routines and avoid going outside. Put simply, to do nothing. War metaphors also tend to be, well, metaphorical. They lack precision and clarity, both of which are in desperately short supply right now.[15]

If a government's goal is to weaken the citizens' sense of democracy, terrorism rather than war would have been a more appropriate metaphor to characterize governments' and the media's attitude to COVID-19: an invisible and lethal enemy, capable of attacking at any moment anywhere, against which only the authorities can save the country. This is exactly the narrative that a 2004 programme aired by the BBC tried to expose about the relationship between terrorism and public policy:

> Increasingly, politicians are seen simply as managers of public life. But now they have discovered a new role that restores their power and authority. Instead of delivering dreams, politicians now promise to protect us from nightmares. They say that they will rescue us from dreadful dangers that we cannot see and do not understand.[16]

In other words, if it is accepted that a virus is spreading rapidly, is dangerous but has a low mortality rate, and that by taking special care people could be relatively safe, they are unlikely to assent to being reduced to a state of long-term self-isolation or to being subjected to police scrutiny in public, or drawn into war against a country because of what it did, or did not do. By contrast, if the public is told that the virus has a high death rate, that it affects not only those with pre-existing health problems but also healthy individuals, and that for the time being there is no prospect of a vaccine or a cure, citizens will be more likely to tolerate the loss of their liberty. In the best case scenario, where there is no actual danger to democracy,

---

14 Friedman 2020.
15 Serhan 2020.
16 Curtis 2004.

Law, rights, and public policy   53

inducing helplessness to facilitate the acceptance of extreme measures can be an effective short-term strategy, but in the long term it is likely to cause unpredictable harm to the public's democratic sensitivities.

Our purpose in these pages is not to analyze the relationship between public policy and security, and the difficulty of distinguishing a conspiracy from a *Realpolitik* scheme inspired by the contemporary iterations of the US perception management programme of the Reagan era[17] or similar exercises by its Eastern counterparts. Actually, this narrative matches almost perfectly the tone of the message broadcast by several democratic countries to support their public security policies. As discussed in Chapter 2, the public policy choices that buttressed the curtailment of civil liberties, have often been influenced, at least at the height of the pandemic when hard decisions were necessary, by a toxic combination of political ignorance and unreliable statistics. We shall never know how many patients died from the virus, how many perished because of the inefficiencies of the public healthcare systems, or how many lost their lives because of deliberate public policy choices about herd immunity or placing economic needs ahead of human life. Having (or lacking) this knowledge matters because statistics and records contributed to the creation of an Armageddon-like atmosphere that influenced the assessment of the crisis and the extent of the restrictions the public was willing to accept.

The pandemic has, however, been a means by which to enhance the enforcement of public security powers and expand political control by ruling parties over their political opponents and dissent. Among the various statutes that expanded police powers, it worth mentioning the United Kingdom's Coronavirus Act 2020.[18] One of the objectives of the legislation is

> to ensure police and immigration officers have the authority to enforce these measures where necessary. Therefore, the bill will enable the police and immigration officers to detain a person, for a limited period, who is, or may be, infectious and to take them to a suitable place to enable screening and assessment.[19]

The Draconian notion that a person may be detained and subjected to medical treatment against their will is reminiscent of the political abuse of psychiatry

---

17 President of the United States 'National Security Decision Directive number 130' 6 March 1984—declassified on 20 December 1991.
18 Parliament of the United Kingdom 'An Act to make provision in connection with coronavirus; and for connected purposes' 25 March 2020.
19 UK Department of Health & Social Care 'What the Coronavirus Bill will do' 26 March 2020. www.gov.uk/government/publications/coronavirus-bill-what-it-will-do/what-the-coronavirus-bill-will-do (Visited 23 May 2020).

54   *Law, rights, and public policy*

in the former Soviet Union and China,[20] yet several European countries have adopted legislation authorizing compulsory medical screening:

> In Europe, Italy is one of the few countries, together with Spain, Sweden and Switzerland, in which compulsory psychiatric admission (CA) can be arranged only when the need for treatment criteria are met (1–6). Most other countries also consider certain danger criteria, with a considerable variability, from potential danger to oneself and others (e.g., France, Germany, Austria, and the Netherlands) to unacceptability for the community (Ireland and Cyprus).[21]

The loss of the freedom of movement and of the body's inviolability implied by COVID-19 mandatory treatment has its cultural roots in the Middle European approach, based on the notion of a 'potential danger' to society as a whole. Without stringent legal protection it has no place in a modern, democratic society.

Free speech and fake news

Another war waged by governments has been the battle against fake news. This has generated further restraints on free speech in the name of containing the spread of false or alarming information about the virus which could undermine public order. Action against those who engage in these activities does not, however, depend on the veracity or otherwise of the information broadcast. Striking examples of the curbing of free speech are not confined to China; attacks on journalists by the police occurred during the protests against the killing of George Floyd in the United States. But a more nuanced approach is required than the Manichean contest between supporting the government by restraining the exercise of free speech, on the one hand, and being perceived as an enemy of the state by criticizing their approach to the virus and the accuracy of the data on which it is based, on the other. Public opinion and legitimate dissent played an important role in exposing the Hungarian anti-Coronavirus fake news legislation passed in March 2020 as a less than subtle restriction of free speech. In principle, it is acceptable to criminalize the spreading of false information that may generate genuine fear and alarm. This applies not only to COVID-19, but also, for example, to false information that affects stock exchange transactions, as is the law in several countries. In the Hungarian case, however, it is the method by which the law was enforced rather than the law itself that disproportionately curtailed civil liberties. 'Government critics say the police action is creating a

---

20   Bonnie 2002: 136–144.
21   Oliva, Ostacoli, Versino, Portigliatti Pomeri, Furlan, Carletto, Picci, Rocco 2018.

Law, rights, and public policy 55

"chilling effect" in a country where many people—especially those outside the capital—are already scared to speak their minds in public'.[22]

Spreading false or unreliable information—fake news—about the Coronavirus is obviously a problem, but hardly a new one. Long before the pandemic several jurisdictions already had in force provisions to penalize the spreading of false information. Section 505(1) of India's 1860 India's Penal Code creates the offence of 'making, publishing or circulating any statement, rumour or report which may cause fear or alarm to the public, or to any section of the public'.[23] Similarly, Article 7 of the Irish Criminal Justice Public Order Act punishes those who 'distribute or display any writing, sign or visible representation which is threatening, abusive, insulting or obscene with intent to provoke a breach of the peace or being reckless as to whether a breach of the peace may be occasioned', as does Article 656 of the Italian Penal Code which penalizes those who spread false, exaggerated or biased news capable of affecting public order. Article 322-14 of the French *Code Pénal* contains similar sanctions, and the Japanese Broadcasting Act has a specific provision that compels broadcasters not to distort facts.[24] Even the Russian Federation has specific legislation that, since 2006, may be used to block the online sharing of information that threatens public safety and provides for the prosecution of those who spread it.[25]

Thus, if the goal is to prevent public disorder by the spreading of Coronavirus-related online fake news, the pandemic did not initiate unfamiliar legislative restrictions on free speech because, yet again, it is the *enforcement* of existing statutes that attempts to strike a reasonable balance between civil liberties and public order. Where freedom is circumscribed it is normally the result of the (sometimes covert) enforcement of these powers rather than their enlargement. From this perspective, then, even in China the virus has not been used as an excuse to tighten the Party's control over the citizen. In fact, the restrictions on free speech related to the pandemic are but another epiphenomenon of the public order principle according to which ideas can circulate as long as they do not lead to crowds protesting on the streets, as described by Ronald Dworkin in his account of an academic visit to China:

> The Communist leaders, several people told me, are very much aware that the Party came to power through mass movements and is likely to

---

22 Bayer 2020.

23 Jain & Singh 2020.

24 Broadcasting Act, Act No. 132 of 1950, amended by Act No. 96 of 2014, art. 4, para. 1, item 3. www.japaneselawtranslation.go.jp/law/detail/?printID=&ft=2&re=02&dn=1&yo =broadcasting&ia=03&ph=&x=0&y=0&ky=&page=1&vm=02 (Visited 3 June 2020).

25 Russian Federation, 'Federal Law 149-FZ of 27 July 2006 on information, informational technologies and the protection of information'. English text available at www.wipo.int/ed ocs/lexdocs/laws/en/ru/ru126en.pdf (Visited 4 June 2020).

56 *Law, rights, and public policy*

lose power only in the same way; it is therefore frightened of any group, even a non-political group like the Falun Gong, that has demonstrated its power to produce mass meetings and demonstrations, or of any publication, like that of The Tiananmen Papers, that threatens to embarrass the present Party leaders and undermine their personal position. But the Party is not frightened of purely academic discussions in which only general philosophical opinions and aspirations are mooted. (When I asked why no attempt was made to interfere with my own lectures, once the tenor of the lectures had become known to the Party members who attended, I was told, with great delicacy, that I seemed incapable of bringing a crowd into the streets.)[26]

Although not as sweeping as the Chinese or Russian approach, the French method raises troubling questions for free expression. The government arrogated to itself the power to decide which source should be considered as a 'reliable' vector of information about the pandemic. In its commendable effort to help the *citoyens* distinguish truth from falsehood, the Ministry of Culture, backed by the *service d'information du gouvernement* (also known as 'SIG'—the branch of the civil service that is responsible for the institutional communications of the government and monitors public opinion), launched an official page entitled '*Désinfox coronavirus*'. It was intended to host 'handpicked' columns published by various French media outlets that, according to the exclusive assessment of the government, delivered reliable information about the virus.

This initiative ignited a protest by the media that accused the government of spreading innuendos among readers about the closeness of the selected media with the executive. Also, as the journalists' union declared, '*l'Etat n'est pas l'arbitre de l'information*'—the State is not the judge of information.[27] It created the impression that by 'whitelisting' certain publications, those excluded from the list were *ipso facto* unreliable. Unable to resist the pressure of the media, the government first announced that an offending report would have been deleted once the pandemic was over, but finally, on 5 May 2020 an official statement of the Ministry of Culture declared the termination of the programme, claiming that it was not the intention of the

---

26 Dworkin 2002: 64–67.
27 Syindacat des journalistes, Syndacat des redacteurs of Arrêt sur images, BFM-TV, Courrier international, *Les Echos*, Europe 1, *Le Figaro*, France 2, France 3 National, France Info, franceinfo.fr, France Inter, Le JDD, *Libération*, M6, Marianne, Mediapart, LCP, *Le Monde*, L'Obs, *Le Parisien*, *Paris Match*, *Le Point*, *Premières Lignes*, *RFI, RMC, RTL, Sud Ouest, Télérama, La Tribune, TV5 Monde, 20 Minutes*, et la Société des personnels de L'Humanité. 'L'Etat n'est pas l'arbitre de l'information', *Le Monde* online edition 3 May 2020. www.lemonde.fr/idees/article/2020/05/03/l-etat-n-est-pas-l-arbitre-de-l-informat ion_6038527_3232.html (Visited 3 June 2020).

Law, rights, and public policy   57

government to establish either control over the media nor to discriminate between different media outlets.[28]

The British reaction to Coronavirus fake news is no less remarkable:

> The government is cracking down on misinformation about the coronavirus pandemic. A rapid response unit within the Cabinet Office is working with social media firms to remove fake news and harmful content. Culture Secretary Oliver Dowden said action was needed 'to stem the spread of falsehoods and rumours, which could cost lives'.[29]

Unlike the French approach, the British did not target the 'official' press but devoted its attention to the 'usual online suspects': trolls, haters, and 'Eastern disinformers'. But no charges were laid against the media. Instead the government took justice into its own hands, and decided what was unlawful, and pronounced its decision by informing social media to remove the offending content. In other words, two of the world's most democratic countries allowed the executive to declare 'State-endorsed truth' in order to protect public safety from alleged illegitimate behaviour without a fair trial. And it is revealing, though coincidental, that in both jurisdictions the task was operated not, as one might expect, by the Home Office or its equivalent, but by the ministries of culture which, in Orwell's *Nineteen Eighty-Four* Newspeak, was dubbed 'Minitrue': the Ministry of Truth!

In its somewhat desperate attempt to empty the sea with a bucket, the British government teamed up with American Big Tech firms:

> Big Tech and government agencies have created task forces to fight coordinated misinformation campaigns. But they are relatively powerless to clamp down on this sort of grassroots, user-created misinformation that has become the bread-and-butter for how falsities spread across social media as fast as the virus itself is jumping from country to country. Tech companies and policymakers are finding that the tens of millions of euros and dollars they have spent to detect, monitor and combat sophisticated digital misinformation campaigns have little effect when regular social media users, and not foreign governments, are the ones spreading falsehoods.[30]

The irony is inescapable. Big Tech which, in the name of free speech refused to restrict users spreading on their platforms any information regardless of

---

28 *Liberation*, 'Le gouvernement supprime son service controversé «Désinfox coronavirus»' 5 May 2020. www.liberation.fr/direct/element/le-gouvernement-supprime-son-service-contr overse-desinfox-coronavirus_113197/ (Visited 3 June 2020).

29 *BBC News* 'Coronavirus: Fake news crackdown by UK government' 30 March 2020. www.bbc.com/news/technology-52086284 (Visited 4 June 2020).

30 Scott 2020.

58 *Law, rights, and public policy*

its credibility, was now actively scrutinizing and combating misinformation, the exploitation of advertising, and fact-checking of financial support.[31]

Free speech advocates might, however, breathe a sigh of relief; this enterprise has been futile:

> A quick search across these platforms still brings up reams of misinformation ... For once, this is not a failure of Big Tech to clamp down on sophisticated—and coordinated—online campaigns to spread fake news. ... Instead, people are sharing rumors, fake stories and half-truths about COVID-19 with each other directly across the likes of Instagram and Twitter as they struggle to understand how best to protect themselves and their families.[32]

But any satisfaction may be premature. The problem is not that Big Tech has failed, but that it decided unilaterally what content to remove, thereby assuming the role of a State or a State-like power, a disturbing development we consider in Chapter 4. And, as if this were not sufficiently troubling, it also funds independent fact-checking organizations. How long it can remain independent is uncertain, especially in view of the generosity of the industry in funding these huge corporations. The reality is that the problem of fake news may be resolved without the need for special legislation. Existing provisions are perfectly adequate and may easily be adapted to deal with the most egregious instances of false, harmful reports. The real issue is that in a democracy there cannot be a general exemption for free speech or other civil liberties. In other words, one cannot invoke the right to privacy, free speech, or other fundamental rights against the State and expect that they are immune to all legal encumbrances. Thus, and this is the only practicable option, it is a matter for the courts to assess whether certain acts warrant protection by weighing individual rights against the public interest.

Clearly this democratic model is a product of less febrile times. The advent of fake news is not simply an Internet meme; it is, in effect, itself a pandemic. One person shares a hoax which then bounces into others' social network profiles or instant messaging accounts. They keep bouncing either because it is amusing or because it is actually believed to be true or because it confirms the conspiracies they regard as valid. Whether the criminality of threats to public order resides in explicit legislation as a collateral effect of other infringements, it should be judged both by reference to its material form and the *mens rea* of the alleged offender. This assessment can, of course, be undertaken only by an independent judge, which obviously

---

31 Kang-Zing, Jin 'Keeping People Safe and Informed About the Coronavirus' Facebook Newsroom 3 June 2020. https://about.fb.com/news/2020/06/coronavirus/ (Visited 8 June 2020).

32 Scott 2020.

Law, rights, and public policy 59

requires time and adequate judicial officers. Is it sensible to charge hundreds of thousands of individuals with spreading fake news?

While, as pointed out, numerous provisions exist to permit courts to penalize the proliferation of false reports, as we have learned from history, what the law permits is not necessarily right or fair. Taking the judicial path means resorting—again—to a 'muscular' solution to (ineffectively) fix a problem of (lack of) culture and education. From this perspective the novelty of the Coronavirus is, yet again, that those who should be censured for broadcasting false information are the very same individuals that these sanctions should protect: ordinary people who are not necessarily criminals. Notwithstanding legal controls, the deluge of fake news is unstoppable by the laws currently available. But that does not imply that the only option is to allow governments to decide what is true or false, or, even worse, to confer this power on private bodies. As the French journalists' unions declared, it is not for the State to police ideas, no matter how wrong or obnoxious; only public education can achieve that end. Resorting to the might of the State violates far more important principles of a democratic society: the separation of powers, judicial review of administrative action, and the right to a fair trial.

Privacy and public safety

Mass data-gathering and surveillance are widely and openly practised in Western countries. Few realize that mobile telephone mast data, together with Internet traffic are mandatorily retained by Internet service providers and made available to law enforcement authorities. These routinely obtain 'website access blocking orders' that are tantamount to global 'interception' of all Internet DNS queries made by users to enforce a selective 'hijack' of the session to prevent it from reaching the desired network resource. Court judgements without the names of the parties anonymized are made public. So too are business databases relating to individuals' creditworthiness. The police maintain an extensive database of individuals' previous involvement in criminal conduct, where (as in Italy since 1931) you may be included merely because you are regarded as a suspect.[33] Similarly (as in the UK) such data may be made available by a Disclosure and Barring Service Check allowing employers to obtain 'spent and unspent convictions, cautions, reprimands and final warnings ... any information held by local police that's considered relevant to the role ... whether the applicant is on the list of

---

33 Article 4 of the Royal Decree 18 June 1931 n. 773: 'L'autorità di pubblica sicurezza ha facoltà di ordinare che le persone pericolose o sospette e coloro che non sono in grado o si rifiutano di provare la loro identità siano sottoposti a rilievi segnaletici'.

60 *Law, rights, and public policy*

people barred from doing the role'.[34] DNA police databases are increasingly attractive to genetic forensic scientists who wish to develop phenotyping methods, and tissue and genetic sequencing biobanks are accessible to researchers. Japanese banks can access police databases to discover whether a loan applicant is a member of a crime syndicate.[35]

It is hard to square the extensive availability of personal information with the hullabaloo about extensive invasions of privacy and the emergence of a police state when many governments resorted to information technology and the Internet to comprehend and contain the pandemic using contact tracing. The right to privacy, it will be suggested below, cannot be treated as sacrosanct in the face of a killer virus. All rights have their limitations, especially when an emergency threatens lives and livelihoods. This is, of course, not to provide *carte blanche* to the executive; every restriction of fundamental rights demands a scrupulous balancing of freedom against public security, safety, or health.

Striking this balance requires an understanding of the relationship between the right to privacy and confronting a pandemic. According to epidemiologists, eradicating an infective disease involves three courses of action: tracking every single infected person, tracing all their contacts, and explaining the eradication programme to the public. These guidelines were adopted during the smallpox pandemic; a disease that, like COVID-19, is spread by droplets. This strategy resulted in the complete eradication in 1980 of the Variola virus: 'When a patient was identified, the address was taken and a house visit was made. If diagnosed as smallpox the patient was then isolated and there was a local vaccination activity—a "containment activity"—with residents of 30 households around that patient vaccinated'.[36]

Apart from vaccines and other specific medical means, contact tracing is indispensable to any virus containment/eradication programme: it is of the utmost importance to retrieve as much information as possible about an infected individual: the places visited, the means of transport used, the individuals or groups contacted, the food consumed, daily habits and the deviations from them, and so on. One of the key strengths of (real) contact tracing is that it does not require computers, software, or the Internet to succeed. It is a slow process like a police investigation rather than a collection of a vast amount of unreliable information to be interpreted later. Nor does 'artificial intelligence' or 'big data' have a role to play other than being promoted in the media as game-changers in the search for a cure. Of course, as with a police investigation, contact tracing is not and cannot be anonymous.

---

34 United Kingdom Government 'Check someone's criminal record as an employer'. www.g ov.uk/dbs-check-applicant-criminal-record (Visited 5 June 2020).

35 Kawakami 2018.

36 Polio Global Eradication Initiative 'Poliovirus vs smallpox containment: An interview with David Heymann' 11 June 2019. http://polioeradication.org/news-post/poliovirus-vs-sma llpox-containment-an-interview-with-david-heymann/ (Visited 8 June 2020).

Law, rights, and public policy 61

But it is important to recognize that it is not simply a matter that touches on the individual's right to privacy, but to the broader questions of personal dignity, the right to health and safety, and the freedom to conduct scientific research and inquiry.

To confuse, or even equate, the right to privacy with data protection frequently results in the latter being conceived as a substitute for the former.[37] In particular, it has engendered misunderstanding about the use of computer programmes to collect and analyze COVID-19-related information. Naturally, 'traditional' contact tracing requires digital technologies, but at least in respect of the search for infected individuals, it is predominantly a human activity. The unrelenting blind faith in digital deities generated widespread claims that 'contact tracing computer programmes' would work faster and better than the 'old' manual systems. As a consequence, several countries experimented with these sorts of software to improve their detection and containment capability. Acting reflexively, privacy practitioners and activists continue to raise a barrage of objections to the use of information technology, in particular the ubiquitous smartphone—to trace infected individuals.

As paradoxical as it may sound, this technology actually tends to create more problems than solutions, hampering Coronavirus elimination efforts. The naive assumption persists that because they are 'computer based' they are somehow superior to the labours of contact tracing, which is a process, not an 'app'. Rigorous contact tracing requires a complex infrastructure and individuals with proper training in locating those infected, understanding the symptoms, performing tests, and diagnosing the condition. China and South Korea, to cite only two examples, have deployed an effective contact tracing strategy shaped according to their individual local laws and exhibiting a rather dissimilar approach. In strictly factual terms, the measures adopted in China are no different from those of other countries in Asia and the rest of the world: quarantine, identification of infected persons, social distancing, and triage when entering a public place, temperature detection, and sanitization. The real difference resides in the way in which these objectives have been achieved, and this is attributable to the strong integration between physical control measures, surveillance technology, and the control of public opinion (China) and transparency (South Korea):

> Contact tracing in China is also carried out by allowing access to premises only after having scanned a QR code that detects the presence in a specific place, having declared his personal details, the fact that he has not been, in the last fourteen days, in the province of Hubei and noted his body temperature. A Health Code system, at the same time, assigns to each person a self-explanatory colour code (green, yellow, red) that

37 Monti & Wacks 2019: 20.

62 *Law, rights, and public policy*

varies according to the places crossed: the (automatic) change from green to yellow implies the automatic quarantine. In the subway, while the loudspeakers obsessively repeat the rules to be respected before entering the carriage, body temperature is detected and it is mandatory to check in via WeChat (the messaging system used in China) in order to declare your presence associated with your mobile phone number, form of transport, coach and time of departure. Another application indicates (anonymously) the places where contagions have been detected, where artificial walls have been installed to prevent people from leaving the house freely, but were forced to pass through specific gates.[38]

The South Korean approach, while superficially similar, is profoundly different as it is supported by a well-founded democratic system that nevertheless allows the police to access the supervised interconnection of the country's huge number of public and private databases. This enables them to 'backtrace' the behaviour of whoever has tested positive for the virus:

> The 2015 MERS outbreak, however, triggered amendments to the Contagious Disease Prevention and Control Act (CDPCA) and, with the amendments, the CDPCA was given authority to override certain provisions of the PIPA and other privacy laws. Thus, under the current CDPCA, public agencies including the Ministry of Health and Welfare (MOHW) and Korea Centers for Disease Control and Prevention (KCDC) can, at the outbreak of a serious infectious disease, collect, profile, and share 7 categories of data (Figure) that pertain to infected individuals or those suspected to be infected. Specifically, the data that can be collected include location data (including location data collected from mobile devices); personal identification information; medical and prescription records; immigration records; card transaction data for credit, debit, and prepaid cards; transit pass records for public transportation; and closed-circuit television (CCTV) footage.[39]

The South Korean experience merits closer examination for at least three reasons.

First, it debunks the myth that mass surveillance is an ineluctable feature of authoritarian regimes and inevitably endangers civil liberties. The extensive use of database and surveillance cameras is conducted under strict compliance with the rule of law and the protection of privacy. Second, it demonstrates a profound understanding of the importance of fundamental rights that translates into a non-automatic restriction 'for the sake of security'. At the start of the contagion, the virus spread rapidly partly because

---

38 Monti 2020: 16–17.
39 Park, Jeehyun, & Ko 2020.

Law, rights, and public policy 63

of the religious group-worshipping practices of a Christian sect, the Church of _Shincheonji_, and its initial opposition to making the names of their followers public to enable them to be tested.[40] In other words, the combined effect of the exercise of two fundamental rights fully recognized by the South Korean legal system, that of religious freedom and privacy, prevented a timely intervention in a major outbreak of infection. Still, the government did not exploit this initial opposition (latterly withdrawn) to call for a crackdown on fundamental rights.

Third, South Korea—like China—has been able to implement an effective contact tracing programme thanks to a truly enormous technological infrastructure. A system which takes many years to achieve. What paid off was a long-term public policy directed at equipping the country with a comprehensive digital transformation.

A similar approach, both in technological and regulatory terms, has been applied in Taiwan:

> Taiwan leveraged its national health insurance database and integrated it with its immigration and customs database to begin the creation of big data for analytics; it generated real-time alerts during a clinical visit based on travel history and clinical symptoms to aid case identification. It also used new technology, including QR code scanning and online reporting of travel history and health symptoms to classify travelers' infectious risks based on flight origin and travel history in the past 14 days. Persons with low risk (no travel to level 3 alert areas) were sent a health declaration border pass via SMS (short message service) messaging to their phones for faster immigration clearance; those with higher risk (recent travel to level 3 alert areas) were quarantined at home and tracked through their mobile phone to ensure that they remained at home during the incubation period.[41]

Comparing the strategies of these countries with those where the 'sound' Western legal tradition obtains, reminds one of the British Locomotive Act of 1865. Metaphorically, in respect of digital technologies, some countries still require that a self-propelled coach should be preceded by a man who 'shall carry a red flag constantly displayed, and shall warn the riders and drivers of horses of the approach of such locomotives, and shall signal the driver thereof when it shall be necessary to stop' and in certain other countries Level 5 autonomous self-driven cars are already a thing of the past!

> Far from being the new frontiers of democracy—and of the technological one, in particular—South Korea and Taiwan have had the merit,

40 Wong 2020.
41 Wang, Ng, Brook 2020.

64   *Law, rights, and public policy*

however, of creating a wider space of reflection and to be deepened on the role of science and technology, compared with the asphyxiated European debate, sclerotized on the dualism 'freedom-safety' or on that which opposes 'privacy' to 'global control' and which sees China as the only interlocutor, beyond which there are the proverbial lions.[42]

Considering the scope and complexity of the Chinese, South Korean, and Taiwanese infrastructures, one might query the efficacy of a simple app, disconnected by a contact tracing unit which depends on the reliability of the individual or, in the best case scenario, of a health professional who authorizes him or her to self-declare as being infected. Despite their name, it is now clear that many computer programmes advertised as 'contact tracing apps' do not do this. They would better be called, following Google and Apple, an 'exposure notification app' as they only warn the user of being or having been in the same location with (or in dangerous proximity to) an infected person. Exposure notification in itself, though, can be executed at different levels of intrusiveness into the public and private life of a subject. The greater the anonymity, the less effective the computer programme.

The problem with exposure notification software is not merely its name, but the difficulties of balancing the right to privacy with pandemic containment and public security preservation. In contrast to actual contact tracing, the 'privacy-oriented exposure notification' only requires matching an individual who has been tested (or self-declared) positive with all those with whom they have contacted, regardless of the location of the encounter. When a person is declared positive to the virus, he or she notifies their status, and the 'system' sends out a warning to all those who are listed as being in unsafe propinquity to the infected. These exposure notifications are performed entirely anonymously—in response to the perceived risks to personal privacy identified by privacy advocates.[43]

A member of the Security Group at the University of Cambridge Computer Laboratory rightly recognizes a number of technical difficulties that involve the effectiveness of contact tracing apps which may be summarized as follows.[44] First, there is the problem of data reliability and accuracy. The 'exposure notification app' is promoted as an effective solution to ascertain whether—and for how long—an individual has been exposed to an infected person. If the 'infected status' is self-assessed, there is a high probability of a relevant number of false positives unless the contagion is declared by a physician who should be the only person permitted to sound

42 Monti 2020.
43 *Amnesty International*, 'Bahrain, Kuwait and Norway contact tracing apps among most dangerous for privacy' 16 June 2020. www.amnesty.org/en/latest/news/2020/06/bahrain-kuwait-norway-contact-tracing-apps-danger-for-privacy/ (Visited 17 July 2020).
44 Anderson 2020.

Law, rights, and public policy 65

the alert. This would reduce to nil the prospect of error or malicious or hoax reports undermining the results. From a 'privacy protection' perspective, though, the price of this choice would be to accept the loss of complete anonymity.

Another matter that might frustrate the reliability of the results is the matching technology itself. The general consensus among 'experts' identified the use of Bluetooth as the preferred method of detecting human-to-human proximity measured by the decay of the signal strength emitted by a smartphone until it reaches another smartphone using the same software. In other words, the smartphone is supposed to launch a microwave that loses strength as it moves further away from the emitting antenna. Measuring this waning signal determines the distance between the two smartphones. But Bluetooth microwaves behave differently according to the material through which they travel: a supermarket cashier might spend days behind a Plexiglas screen, or a researcher might be separated by a wall from the next room where classes are being held, yet they would be included on the list of those that might have been in contact with a Coronavirus carrier:

> I expect the app developers will have to fit a user interface saying 'You're within range of device 38a5f01e20. Within infection range (y/n)?' But what happens when people get an avalanche of false alarms? They learn to click them away. A better design might be to invite people to add a nickname and a photo so that contacts could see who they are. 'You are near to Ross [photo] and have been for five minutes. Are you maintaining physical distance?'[45]

Would that be viable? Perhaps, but this adds yet another layer of complication to the management of the software, the risk of creating (false) alarms and, again, a further loss of anonymity.

To summarize, the difference in the goals of these strategies sets the difference in the information that is collected. Contact tracing requires the collection of as much data and personal information as possible and allows exposure notification and infected-places warnings. Doing the opposite is not possible, as collecting the subset of information needed to execute the two latter activities is not enough for a complete contact tracing activity. Moreover, blind faith in technology assumes that if a person is fully tracked in his or her movement and contacts, the need for a human check is eliminated. Not all individuals who come into contact with the virus-spreader might have a smartphone, also if they have one it does not register whether the exposure notification software is active or working, and even whether the software programme works, it may be prone to a high number of false positives. There is also the problem that the efficacy exposure notification

45 Ibid.

66 *Law, rights, and public policy*

software depends on how it interacts with the rest of the public health system and the social conditions of the individuals concerned. Lastly, security vulnerabilities and bugs[46] can reduce the effectiveness of the results.

It is paradoxical that from an EU perspective, to 'protect the right to privacy' exposure notification software violates data protection regulations that require the data controller to ensure that personal information is processed so as to guarantee its reliability in the safeguarding of fundamental rights, including, of course, life. In other words: it is not (or it should not be) possible to enforce excessive levels of anonymity if that choice endangers the reliability of the processing as required by the EU General Data Protection Regulation (GDPR) and, thus, the overall the efficiency of the Coronavirus containment efforts. A similar concern relates to the use of smartphones as conduits to enforce geo-fencing-based quarantine, real time geolocation, and warnings about the presence of the virus in certain locations as a complement of a global containment strategy. All of these goals can be achieved with different levels of anonymity but, strictly speaking, they are really intended to prevent the spreading of the virus rather than contact tracing. This difference is irrelevant, however, in respect of the balancing of individual rights.

By adding location tracking to exposure notification the app can provide an 'infected place warning' that complements the containment strategy and a subset of contact tracing. By providing a map of where the infection has been detected, people can avoid potentially hazardous places, but authorities may receive a 'real time quarantine infringement notification' and react in different ways, ranging from automated warnings to the police to detain the offender. Many of the perplexities expressed about the way the exposure notification should work remain pertinent. Of course geo-fencing and geolocation can be executed on a voluntary and anonymous basis. But without control of the reliability of the information released by individuals, it becomes almost impossible to avoid the mischievous designation of a certain location (for instance, a wealthy suburb) as a Coronavirus hotbed. The alternative would be to allow only infected location data released from official sources, with the risk that the State itself would process the information in order to 'nudge' people into staying clear of explicit areas.

Moreover, geo-fencing and geolocation can be designed to work passively, so that the software programme does not associate the location of the individual with his or her identity, limiting the outcomes to private and personal use and sharing (provided that this is possible) only his or her whereabouts anonymously. But, yet again, this requires a trade-off: knowing that a potential Coronavirus vector appeared in a specific place but disregarding the individual's identity prevents the health system from intervening in a timely manner. More complicated design layers can be superimposed to

46 Williams 2020.

protect the right to privacy, such as making the personal identity of the virus vector known only to the particular law enforcement officers that need to detain him or her. But it is clear that the more personal identity is hidden (or even lost) the less useful are the data. And the more citizens are shielded by comprehensive monitoring, the less effectively the authorities can manage the contagion.

Many of these problems, and in particular those related to the relationship between privacy and safety, arise from a 'black-or-white' presentation of the argument according to which one is either protected against the infection or the right to privacy is protected. Privacy has regrettably become something of a fetish, and policymakers need to ask the always uncomfortable question whether we are willing to accept a non-trivial limitation of democratic freedom by venerating this totem, which like the Phoenix Arab of Pietro Metastasio everyone says exists, but no one knows where! In fact, contact tracing and exposure notification, geo-fencing and in general the use of citizen-generated data to manage the crisis is not only related to their impact on personal privacy. Privacy is a fundamental right which we, as authors, have devoted much of our professional lives to analyzing, promoting, and defending. It is not, however, an über-right that trumps all others—especially during a deadly pandemic. Safeguarding personal information vouchsafes respect for human dignity. If the State is obliged to violate a person's intimate sphere to establish whether he or she has been infected and to whom he or she may have passed on the virus, the primary concern is to ensure that this individual does not suffer discrimination as a plague-spreader. For example, in Italy a nurse received mail at her home accusing her of spreading the disease because she worked in a hospital.[47] Her privacy was not in issue; the dignity of her work and individual sacrifice was affronted by malevolence. Yet the obsession with privacy has all but been obliterated by other individual and community interests and rights. This has meant, for instance, that arguments such as the social cost of 'muscular' public security as a substitute for comprehensive technology-based monitoring has found no space. This might be explained by the cultural and infrastructural failure to embed technology into the public policy process:

> The difference between the South Korean approach and that of European countries doesn't represent the simple cliché of eastern collectivism versus western individualism. In fact, information exposure can prevent the need for a lockdown of individuals' movements. In this way, governments around the world are facing a hard choice between these two violations of individual rights (information exposure and movement restriction). South Korea has chosen the former, but France and Italy had to choose the latter. The former requires the necessary

47 Montanari 2020.

68 *Law, rights, and public policy*

infrastructure and a culture that tolerates a certain level of surveillance, neither of which can be created overnight.[48]

But, while this observation is germane, it is not necessarily true that the policy choices of various governments have either been impeded by the reluctance to violate competing rights or tolerated because of cultural acceptance of surveillance.[49] In fact, when a State curtails one right (privacy) to protect another (public safety) it is not committing a violation but an exercise in balancing rival claims. The outcome may be satisfactory, imperfect, or wholly wrong, but rights are not inexorably infringed in this process. The real breach lies in the enforcement of the provisions adopted in order to defeat the pandemic. The COVID-19 experience has revealed that—as in every emergency—power is exercised by those who, at a given time and place, have the capacity to impose it according their will. In the case of the pandemic, it may be distasteful that the State should have access to whatever information is needed to eradicate the virus, find a cure, and care for the infected, and so on. But this is the reality. Nevertheless, of course, the authorities must be accountable for what it does with this information. There is no right to privacy that could preclude a national health service from collecting personal data in its attempt to suppress the contagion. Instead, there is a critical requirement in the EU that personal data are processed according to a need-to-know as prescribed by the General Data Protection Regulation (GDPR). It is also obviously essential that the public trusts the process of information-gathering, and is confident that their personal information will not be abused.

As has been argued several times in these pages, the law has only limited significance during an emergency. This is largely because judicial review of the enforcement of legal provisions is too slow to assure people of the legitimacy of the authority's decisions. In a democracy, this can be achieved by placing on the scales the weight of institutional trustworthiness which persuades the public that it is participating in a common endeavour. In other words, in desperate times when the need for swift action precludes an exhaustive assessment of all the legal implications of public policy, a citizen can only trust the State to cleave to the values of freedom and democratic rights. This can be achieved, as the Japanese scholars Takahashi Ikuo, Arimoto Mayu, and Kurokawa Mariko suggest in relation to contact tracing (or, as it is called in Japan, contact confirmation), by adopting a five-part process in designing a balanced, privacy-conscious, public policy.

1. Acceleration of the evolution toward a digital infrastructure of various government services, including support through digitalization of

---

48 Sonn 2020.
49 The claim that Far East societies are more tolerant of surveillance is examined in Chapter 5.

Law, rights, and public policy   69

contact confirmation, as an integral part of the government's digital transformation enabling programme.

2. Adoption of fact-based policy decisions on privacy awareness with a trade-offs approach.
3. Promotion of fact-based personal information voluntary sharing based on incentive and rewards,
4. Adoption of mechanisms for ensuring privacy in government agencies and checking for their compliance.
5. Execution of a privacy impact assessment on the concerned public infrastructures.[50]

Although this proposal is tailored to Japanese public policy, it is a valuable starting point from which to build a trusted, citizen-oriented entrenching of digital technologies in the public sector without the need to resort to authoritarian methods. If, in regard to public policy, there is a lesson to be learnt from the pandemic it is that the authority-based public policy model in a global health emergency does not work as it once did in other fields such as terrorism or natural disasters. During a pandemic it is both undesirable and impracticable to coerce a population into acquiescence.

Governments and fundamental rights

Public order legislation did not prevent France from deploying an iron fist to deal with the *gilet-jaune* protest that in 2018 culminated in vandalism and the burning down of public buildings and other property.[51] Austria enforced its border protection against the tide of migrants by deploying the military.[52] Since 1931 Italian police have had the power to stop and search anyone and enter their details into the public security database.[53] The way the pandemic has been presented, governments and the media produced disparate reactions. National culture played an important role in addressing the legal issues raised. While it is difficult to draw general conclusions or to compare how legal systems and civil societies of different jurisdictions responded to the crisis, an empirical analysis can provide a partial account of the various approaches.

In pursuit of a quick solution, an essentially political need, certain governments have displayed a questionable attitude toward the enforcement of the rule of law. Curtailing individual liberty in the ostensible defence of public health some, like Hungary, have sacrificed the constitutional rights of citizens by establishing stringent regulatory controls over individuals, portraying

---

50 Takahashi, Arimoto, & Kurokawa 2020.
51 Bouchez 2020.
52 Romano 2017.
53 Article 4 of the Royal Decree 18 June 1931 n. 773 verbatim reads: 'L'autorità di pubblica sicurezza ha facoltà di ordinare che le persone pericolose o sospette e coloro che non sono in grado o si rifiutano di provare la loro identità siano sottoposti a rilievi segnaletici'.

70 *Law, rights, and public policy*

individual rights as legalistic pedantry that thwarts governments from doing 'the right thing'. Italy issued a plethora of confused regulations that raise a number of fundamental constitutional questions; it also deployed a massive police and military apparatus trying, without much success, to impose the quarantine orders with a 'muscular' exercise in public order. In Canada 'a patchwork legal regime has been revealed of new public order laws written on the fly to demand and enforce massive behavioural change'.[54]

The United Kingdom encountered obstacles in the path of proposed Draconian measures thanks to the traditional British respect for individual liberty, but has resorted to dubious 'scientific' theories to nudge citizens, with indifferent results into compliance.[55] The United States did not resort to the President's executive powers, allowing state governors to issue stay-at-home orders, but the White House tried to assert its exclusive right to decide when and how to ease the restrictions.[56] In India, the timely enforced containment measures[57] and the resort to soft power[58] did not prevent police compelling compliance by the use of force.[59],[60] China adopted its normal strategy: 'Confucian' acquiescence and, as a backup, coercion. Taiwan and South Korea relied upon strong social responsibility and governmental transparency without the need for authorities to demonstrate their power to achieve compliance, and the general acceptance of a substantial use of information technology powered contact tracing. By contrast, Thailand and other Far Eastern countries succeeded in containing the virus without resorting to futuristic technology:

> Thailand's low rate of infection appears to be shared by other countries in the Mekong River basin. Vietnam has not recorded a single death and has logged about three months without a case of community transmission. Myanmar has confirmed 336 cases of the virus, Cambodia 166 and Laos just 19.[61]

Germany faced a novel extension of the Health Ministry's powers in response to constitutional intricacies that did not afford the federal government the

---

54 Brean 2020.
55 Sodha 2020.
56 *New York Times* 'Trump Insists He Has "Total" Authority to Supersede Governors' 13–21 April 2020. www.nytimes.com/2020/04/13/us/coronavirus-updates.html (Visited 20 May 2020).
57 Ministry of Information & Broadcasting 'India's response to COVID outbreak' 28 March 2020. https://pib.gov.in/PressReleasePage.aspx?PRID=1608727 (Visited 20 May 2020).
58 Singh 2020.
59 Sircar 2020.
60 *Reuters Now*, 'Indian police use violence against lockdown offenders' 25 March 2020. www.reuters.com/video/watch/idPqZx?now=true (Visited 20 May 2020).
61 Beech, Hannah, 'No One Knows What Thailand Is Doing Right, but So Far It's Working', *The New York Times* online edition 16 July 2020. www.nytimes.com/2020/07/16/world/asia/coronavirus-thailand-photos.html?campaign_id=2&emc=edit_th_20200717&instance_id=20379&nl=todaysheadlines&regi_id=65106828&segment_id=33622&user_id=bf1ee56a5f24018fd37d2b8d31aacf5c (Visited 22 July 2020).

Law, rights, and public policy   71

power to declare a state of emergency. Still, no police state was established: 'the authoritarian temptation is there, it's powerfully tangible—but the liberal counterweight is no less so'.[62] Northern European countries approached their citizens in a pragmatic, non-threatening manner neatly expressed by the words of the Swedish Prime Minister and of the King of the Netherlands: [63]

> Corona has unleashed an incredible amount of positive energy, creativity and public-spiritedness. These are the qualities we will be needing not only for the time being, but certainly also later on should things get even more challenging. Despite public life coming to a grinding halt, you are the ones who are keeping the heart of our society beating. Alertness, solidarity and kindness: as long as we can sustain these qualities we will be able to tackle this crisis together, even if it lasts for some time.[64]

Cultural differences apart, the legal responses in the management of public order and security of the various countries show significant differences as well as some common factors. Safety concerns generated by an invisible and ubiquitous pathogenic agent resulted in a generally quiescent public willing—at least initially—to tolerate significant restrictions on traditional freedoms. Again, the problem is not the 'special powers' in themselves, but in the way they are justified and enforced.

There are several illuminating examples of the problems caused by the deferment of the immediate enforcement of governments' special powers to police authorities.

A French journalist was checked twice at different times on the same day: in one case he was not fined because presenting his journalist badge was enough for the patrol to wave him on, but in the other he was fined because, according to the police officer, the journalist badge was insufficient![65] In Italy, unless the infringement is committed by an infected citizen, violating the quarantine order is an administrative and not automatically a criminal offence. This means that the police can only issue a ticket but have no power of detention. One may question the logic of this choice and query the use of a provision that does not allow its immediate enforcement. Nevertheless, a helicopter of the *Arma dei Carabinieri* (one of the three main Italian law enforcement authorities) was used to generate a sand tornado to force a

---

62 Steinbeis 2020.
63 The Government of Sweden 'The Government's work in response to the virus responsible for COVID-19'. www.government.se/?id=487b9112-00090226-529882e2&in=28&out=87 (Visited 29 May 2020).
64 Royal House of The Netherlands 'Speech by His Majesty the King in light of the coronavirus'. www.royal-house.nl/documents/speeches/2020/03/20/speech-by-his-majesty-the-king-in-light-of-the-coronavirus 20 March 2020 (Visited 24 May 2020).
65 *Le Figaro* 'Coronavirus : de nouvelles sanctions en cas de non-respect du confinement' online edition 22 March 2020. www.lefigaro.fr/politique/coronavirus-de-nouvelles-sanctions-en-cas-de-non-respect-du-confinement-20200322 (Visited 20 May 2020).

72 *Law, rights, and public policy*

man who was standing alone on a beach in Sicily to leave without ascertaining the reason for his presence—because the law stipulated that he was in breach of the law.[66]

The situation in Romania is of particular interest. According to the magazine *Balkan Insight* 'Prime Minister Ludovic Orban ... did ask police officers to avoid fining people unless "the violation is very clear, very severe"'.[67] This may have been a lapse, because none of the EU member States allow police forces the discretion to decide whether or not to report a violation and, more importantly, this was under the direct instruction from the executive. Still, the Romanian prime minister's statement is revealing of the thinness of the ice on which we are skating.

Other examples could be mentioned, but in general the problem is well summarized by Lord Sumption, former judge of the UK Supreme Court:

> The tradition of policing in this country is that policemen are citizens in uniform, they are not members of a disciplined hierarchy operating just at the government's command. ... The police have no power to enforce ministers' preferences but only legal regulations which don't go anything like as far as the government's guidance ... This is what a police state is like. It's a state in which the government can issue orders or express preferences with no legal authority and the police will enforce ministers' wishes.[68]

Lord Sumption's asseveration encapsulates several issues concerning the rule of law and the tension between Parliament, the executive, and the judiciary. While, in theory, every country agrees about the effective measures to contain the spread of the contagion, their actual enforcement varies according to the discretion of the police or—worse—to a single detachment of officers. But there is more to this situation than meets the eye; it exposes the limits of the rule of law in an emergency. It is not that we slide into what some rashly stigmatize as a police state; the danger lies in the creation of two discrete legal systems: one (formally) founded on the law, and the other (de facto) based on the achievement of policy objectives regardless of legal constraints.

---

66 *Il Fatto Quotidiano* 'Coronavirus, viola i divieti e prende il sole in spiaggia a Palermo: allontanato dall'elicottero dei carabinieri' *Il Fatto Quotidiano* Online Edition 11 Aprile 2020. www.ilfattoquotidiano.it/2020/04/11/coronavirus-viola-i-divieti-e-prende-il-sole -in-spiaggia-a-palermo-allontanato-dallelicottero-dei-carabinieri/5767604/ (Visited 20 May 2020).

67 *Stirile TV* 'Ludovic Orban: Am solicitat să nu se de amendă din prima, ci să existe întâi un avertisment' 21 April 2020. http://stiri.tvr.ro/ludovic-orban-la-tvr-am-solicitat-sa-nu-se-de -amenda-din-prima-ci-sa-existe-intai-un-avertisment_860145.html#view (Visited 20 May 2020).

68 *BBC News* 'Coronavirus: Lord Sumption brands Derbyshire Police "disgraceful"' BBC News online 30 March 2020. www.bbc.com/news/uk-england-derbyshire-52095857 (Visited 20 May 2020).

Law, rights, and public policy 73

It is not a case of Ernst Fraenkel's Nazi 'Dual State' where the *Normative State* is 'an administrative body endowed with elaborate powers for safeguarding the legal order as expressed in statutes, decisions of the courts, and activities of the administrative agencies' and the *Prerogative State*: 'that governmental system which exercises unlimited arbitrariness and violence unchecked by any legal guarantees'.[69] The culture and institutions of a sophisticated legal system and a functioning judiciary avert this incubus. But in the Coronavirus condition of 'suspended justice' with most courts in lockdown, the judiciary is incapable of exercising timely control over the abuse of executive power. It should not be forgotten that the retreat of judges from 'interfering' with the enforcers of the Prerogative State (the Gestapo), was instrumental in the transition to totalitarianism in Nazi Germany.[70]

> [J]udges ... later reluctantly yielded to political pressure and finally denied judicial review of all acts of the Gestapo, ie., the instrument of the Prerogative State ... Jus cogens ceased to be binding on the police. ... Even the principle of res judicata was abandoned by the Berlin Court of Appeals, the Bavarian Supreme Court, and the People's Court (the first and last court in cases of high treason), although the Reich Supreme Court adhered to it as late as 1938.[71]

While it is true that the suspension of courts during the pandemic has no political basis, it is difficult not to sense a shift toward Fraenkel's model that, in contrast with an explicit police State, preserves the external appearance of democracy, actually paves the way to authoritarianism. Dictatorships might not *per se* be anti-democratic because every Western legal system (including the Roman Republic) already provides for—or is able to regulate—an emergency where extreme powers are granted to the executive: 'If the constitution of a state is democratic, every exceptional suspension of democratic principles, every exercise of power autonomously from the consent of the majority of those governed can be called dictatorship'.[72]

One might challenge the appropriateness of the term 'dictatorship' to characterize the emergency powers of a prime minister, but semantic hairsplitting apart, there are three questions that should be asked to test whether a democracy is at risk: how slack are the reins given to the executive, for how long, and who (if anyone) has the effective ability to tighten them. Maintaining public order subjects a legal and political system to a political stress test: it is a task that has at its core the need for rapid intervention that

---

69 Fraenkel 1941: xiii. We consider this question further in Chapter 5.
70 Some judges of the Third Reich were, in fact, prosecuted in the so-called 'Justice Trial' at Nuremberg. On the role and moral responsibility of the judiciary when faced with excessive executive powers or injustice, see Wacks 1984, 1991, 1995, 1998, 2000, and 2009.
71 Guradze 1942: 604.
72 Schmitt 1921.

74 *Law, rights, and public policy*

cannot always wait for legislation to be enacted or for a court to issue an order. Each jurisdiction has, of course, its own approach, but a few principles transcend the singularities. The first and the most important is that the power of arrest or the limitations imposed on individual liberty are possible only under a specific (and, ideally, well designed) provision. The question then becomes how swiftly the courts are able to react to abuses of power. Oddly enough, no legislation has been passed to permit a court to intercede on its own volition to check the abuse of public security powers. Second, even in jurisdictions like Italy where crime prevention together with public order and criminal investigation powers are regulated differently,[73] there is always a magistrate tasked to review the way in which law enforcement bodies interpret the law. This means that there is no opportunity for the government or a single minister to issue their own legal interpretation—it is ultimately a matter for the court. Third, the issuing of a ticket for non-compliance with the lockdown measures is ineffective. The principal goal should be the removal of the danger or, in other words, the opportunity for the police to compel compliance and defuse a risky situation, if necessary by physical coercion. But if the legislature fails to enact a Draconian statute of this kind, the police ought not to have the power physically to impose 'go home', or 'crowd dispersing' orders.

Fourth, even if such legislation were passed (or is already in force), how is it to be enforced? By mass arrests? By loading violators into sealed railway carriages to a detention camp or a lazaret? Or by using the dispersal techniques so *en vogue* not only in Far East 'democracies'? Italy proposed an 'old school' version of this last method. This idea was adopted in the United Kingdom with the introduction in mid-September 2020 of so-called COVID marshals. These officials, like the (now aborted) Assistenti Civici, lack genuine power, but may issue 'gentle warnings' to those flouting the rules.[74] The Italian proposal, announced in May 2020, envisaged the establishment of an 'army' of 60,000 souls enlisted from among unemployed and laid-off workers to act as—this was its initially proposed name—the 'Civic Guard'.[75] Following criticism of the idea, the name and purpose of these patrols was nudged into 'Civic Assistants' tasked politely to invite those who do not comply with the containment measures to change their

---

73 In Italy, crime prevention and public order laws are still based on the Royal Decree of the Fascist-era: the Royal Decree of 18 June 1931 n. 773. The suspicion of a police officer suffices for the suspect to be questioned and to produce a State ID or issue a 'do or do not' order that must immediately be obeyed, with no questions asked. In contrast, when police forces act under the public prosecutor's guidance they are bound to comply with the requirements of a fair trial, court supervised approach.

74 www.bbc.com/news/explainers-54105672 (Visited 15 September 2020).

75 ADNKronos 'Federpol: "No a guardie civiche su base volontaria"' 26 May 2020. www. adnkronos.com/lavoro/norme/2020/05/26/federpol-guardie-civiche-base-volontaria_Kj koTRQJkoKyx8ehkzdtrL.html (Visited 28 May 2020).

Law, rights, and public policy 75

behaviour. Civic Assistants are not supposed to have police-like powers, but cutting through the word-weaving, they act as violator-spotters nonetheless. In other words, de facto, they cooperate in maintaining public order under the authority of the President of the Ministries' Council by way of the Civil Protection Department, even though they lack such formal powers. This is a rather bizarre option, considering that the Cabinet is not supposed to have under its exclusive control an organized body whose members, largely uneducated, are distributed throughout the whole country.

Even though times are different and there is, of course, no direct connection, it is impossible not to hear echoes of the reasons (protecting public order) that in 1931 justified the creation of the *Milizia volontaria per la sicurezza nazionale*, the paramilitary wing of the Fascist Party under the direct control of the President of the Ministries' Council (Mussolini himself.) The *Guardie Civiche* case provides several insights about the general issue of the impact of the pandemic on the management of public order. The first and the most obvious is the inability of some governments to conceive of a public order and security model not inspired by a 'muscular' approach. It is of little importance that these Civic Assistants are not accorded police powers. What matters is that the first solution that came to mind was to 'fight' the widespread infringement of the containment measures. This is a study in strength rather than in an alternative based on creative, sensible solutions. One may not entirely agree[76] with those who advocate the end of policing.[77] Still it is fairly clear that improved relationships between police and community increases the prospects of compliance, and not only to criminal provisions.

The second aspect questions the validity itself of a fine-grained approach to COVID-19 provisions' violations to frighten, rather than persuade, citizens to comply. Many countries imposed monetary fines—and even immediate arrest or detention—in cases of the breach of containment provisions. Still, the public order paradox exposed by the COVID-19 is that the actual target of the COVID-19 fine-based policing is the whole population and not a smaller (even though numerous) group of protesters.

The disturbances that erupted across the United States following the death of George Floyd at the hands of the police on 25 May 2020 in Minneapolis are instructive. Public outrage added salt to a wound that has never healed.[78] It turned protests into riots. Many joined the demonstrations in more than 20 States, and fearing that the situation might escalate out of control, the President threatened to read the Insurrection Act of 1807 (lately amended to cope with public order matters) and call up the military.[79]

76 Yglesias 2020.
77 Vitale 2018.
78 Porter 2020.
79 Horton 2020.

76 *Law, rights, and public policy*

Demonstrations comprising a substantial number of people are susceptible to the 'traditional' public order approach. When the entire population is involved, however, brute force cannot suffice. In other words, COVID-19 disrupted the conventional balance between law-abiding citizens (the majority) and 'criminals' or 'offenders' (numerous, but still very limited in number). Protection against those who are infected generates a very different kind of challenge. Moreover, the surge of people flooding into streets and squares in cities and towns once the lockdown has been lifted, even partially, renders it impracticable to arrest or 'deport' all those that violate the law. In other words, when the number of 'delinquents' becomes too large, treating them as criminals to be fined is highly unrealistic. And if only some are punished while others are not, it becomes a major source of injustice.

Third, many countries (at least those that are supposedly democratic) unable to 'think different' than the usual 'muscular' public security mind-set, face an insurmountable obstacle when confronted with the necessity to curb fundamental rights. It is worth pointing out that the very same technology that facilitates mass control of citizens can be adapted to control the manner in which special powers are applied by the executive. This is possible at street level by broadening the use of bodycams and other police behaviour tracing platforms, at the administrative level by tracking every phase of a decisional process, and at the judicial level by promoting the effective use of information technology in courts. In a state of emergency control over the executive would be sufficiently swift to discourage a government to take shortcuts enabled by the delay of the reaction of the judiciary.

Fourth, it is worth asking whether the use of information and telecommunication technologies coupled with a panopticon approach have offered an alternative solution to the challenge of ensuring compliance. The answer would appear to be negative; at least in respect of the conventional manner that technology is associated with security. Indeed, information and telecommunications technologies have been integrated into their usual security management framework to enhance surveillance capabilities. We therefore see the use of drones, digital (video) cameras, and attempts (with various degree of success) to track the movement of every citizen by way of 'contact tracing' software programmes, but we have not fully grasped their effects. This matter is further pursued in Chapter 4.

References

Anderson, Ross. 2020. 'Contact Tracing in the Real World', *Light Blue Touchpaper*, 12 April. www.lightbluetouchpaper.org/2020/04/12/contact-tracing-in-the-real-world/ (Visited 3 June 2020).

Bayer, Lili. 2020. 'Orbán Critics Fall Foul of Hungary's Controversial Corona Law', Politico, online edition, 15 April. www.politico.eu/article/viktor-orban-critics-fall-foul-of-hungary-controversial-coronavirus-covid19-law/ (Visited 23 May 2020).

Law, rights, and public policy 77

Bobbitt, Philip. 2008. *Terror and Consent*. London: Penguin Books.

Bonnie, Richard. 2002. 'Political Abuse of Psychiatry in the Soviet Union and in China: Complexities and Controversies', *Journal of the American Academy of Psychiatry and the Law* 30(1): 136–144.

Bouchez, Yann. 2020. '"Gilets jaunes": jusqu'à trois ans ferme pour l'incendie de la préfecture de Haute-Loire', *Le Monde*, online edition, 10 March. www.l emonde.fr/societe/article/2020/03/10/gilets-jaunes-jusqu-a-trois-ans-ferme-pour-l-incendie-de-la-prefecture-de-haute-loire_6032415_3224.html (Visited 23 May 2020).

Brady, James. 2020. 'USA Press Briefing Room "Remarks by President Trump, Vice President Pence, and Members of the Coronavirus Task Force in Press Briefing"', 16 April. www.whitehouse.gov/briefings-statements/remarks-president-trump-v ice-president-pence-members-coronavirus-task-force-press-briefing-27/ (Visited 20 May 2020).

Brean, Joseph. 2020. 'It's Not Just Civil Liberties. Many Other Charter Rights Have Been Violated in COVID-19 Pandemic', *National Post*, online edition. https://na tionalpost.com/news/its-not-just-civil-liberties-many-other-charter-rights-have-been-violated-in-covid-19-pandemic (Visited 20 May 2020).

Curtis, Adam. 2004. 'The Power of Nightmare. Part 1: Baby it's Cold Outside', *BBC Two*, 20 October.

De Becker, Gavin. 1997. *The Gift of Fear*. New York: Dell Publishing.

De Bernardi, Alberto. 2020. 'Arcuri distorce la storia paragonando il Coronavirus alla guerra', *Il Riformista*, 26 April. www.ilriformista.it/arcuri-distorce-la-storia -paragonando-il-coronavirus-alla-guerra-87645/ (Visited 20 May 2020).

Dittmer, Lowell. 1977. ' Political Culture and Political Symbolism: Toward a Theoretical Synthesis',*World Politics* 29(4): 552–583.

Dworkin, Ronald. 2002. 'Taking Rights Seriously in Beijing', *New York Review of Books* 14(26): 64–67.

Fraenkel, Ernst. 1941. *The Dual State. A Contribution to the Theory of Dictatorship*. New York: Oxford University Press.

Friedman, Thomas. 2020. 'Is Sweden Doing Right?', *New York Times*, 28 April. www.nytimes.com/2020/04/28/opinion/coronavirus-sweden.html (Visited 20 May 2020).

Gargiulo, Martina. 2018. 'Uscire dalla catastrofe. La città di Napoli fra guerra aerea e occupazione alleata', *Diacronie. Studi di Storia Contemporanea* 33(1): 'Guerra e Pace' 29 March. https://journals.openedition.org/diacronie/7187 (Visited 20 May 2020).

Guradze, Heinz. 1942. 'Review of Ernst Fraenkel, The Dual State: A Contribution to the *Theory of Dictatorship*', *Washington University Law Review* 27(4): 603–607.

Hanson, Elaine and Vogel, Gwen 2012. 'The Impact of War on Civilians' in *Trauma Counseling: Theories and Interventions*. New York: Springer Publishing, p. 412.

Hobbes, Thomas. 1651. *Leviathan, or The Matter, Forme, & Power of a Common-Wealth Ecclesiastical and Civil*. London: Andrew Crooke.

Horton, Jake. 2020. 'George Floyd: Can President Trump Deploy the Military?', *BBC Reality Check*, 4 June. www.bbc.com/news/world-us-canada-52893540 (Visited 4 June 2020).

Jain, Khushbu and Brijesh Singh. 'View: Disinformation in Times of a Pandemic, and the Laws around it', 3 April. https://economictimes.indiatimes.com/new s/politics-and-nation/view-disinformation-in-times-of-a-pandemic-and-the-la

78 Law, rights, and public policy

ws-around-it/articleshow/74960629.cms?utm_source=contentofinterest&utm_medium=text&utm_campaign=cppst (Visited 3 June 2020).

Johnson, Mark. 1987. *The Body in the Mind: The Bodily Basis of Meaning, Imagination, and Reason*. Chicago: University of Chicago Press.

Kanter, Johnathan and Katherine Manbeck. 2020. 'COVID-19 Could Lead to an Epidemic of Clinical Depression, and the Health Care System Isn't Ready for That, Either', *The Conversation*, 1 April. https://theconversation.com/covid-19-could-lead-to-an-epidemic-of-clinical-depression-and-the-health-care-system-isnt-ready-for-that-either-134528 (Visited 20 May 2020).

Kawakami, Akihiro 2018. 'Banks Can Now Use NPA Database to Check if Loan Applicants Belong to Criminal Syndicate', *Mainichi Shinbun*, online edition, 4 January. https://mainichi.jp/english/articles/20180104/p2a/00m/0na/017000c (Visited 5 June 2020).

King, Martin Luther Jr. 1963. 'Martin Jr. "Letter from a Birmingham Jail"', 16 April. www.africa.upenn.edu/Articles_Gen/Letter_Birmingham.html (Visited 23 May 2020).

Kirmayer, Lawrence.1988. 'Word Magic and the Rhetoric of Common Sense: Erickson's Metaphors for Mind', *International Journal of Clinical and Experimental Hypnosis* 36(3): 157–172.

Montanari, Laura. 2020. 'Lucca, infermiera trova biglietto nella posta: "Ci porti il Covid"', *La Repubblica*, online edition, 22 April. https://firenze.repubblica.it/cronaca/2020/04/22/news/lucca_infermiera_trova_biglietto_nella_posta_ci_por ti_il_covid_-254727207/ (Visited 20 May 2020).

Monti, Andrea. 2020. 'Science, Techno-Control and Public Policy in the COVID-19 Era', *Quarterly Journal of Administration Science*. Studies on Social Theory and Research Issue 2. https://doi.org/10.32049/RTSA.2020.2.12.

Monti, Andrea and Raymond Wacks. 2019. *Protecting Personal Information: The Right to Privacy Reconsidered*. Oxford: Hart Publishing.

Oliva, Francesco, Luca Ostacoli, Elisabetta Versino, Portigliatti Pomeri, Alberto Furlan, Pier Maria, Carletto Sara, Picci Luigi Rocco. 2018. 'Compulsory Psychiatric Admissions in an Italian Urban Setting: Are They Actually Compliant to the Need for Treatment Criteria or Arranged for Dangerous Not Clinical Condition?', *Frontiers in Psychiatry* 9(740). www.frontiersin.org/articles/10.3389/fpsyt.2018.00740/full (Visited 23 May 2020).

Park, Sangchul, Gina Jeehyun Choi and Haksoo Ko. 2020. 'Information Technology-Based Tracing Strategy in Response to COVID-19 in South Korea—Privacy Controversies', *Journal of the American Medical Association* 323(21): 2129. doi:10.1001/jama.2020.6602.

Porter, Eduardo. 2020. *American Poison. How Racial Hostility Destroyed Our Promise*. New York: Alfred A Knops.

Romano, Luca. 2017. 'Migranti, l'Austria dà l'avvio ai controlli mirati ai confini', Il Giornale, online edition, 10 August. www.ilgiornale.it/news/cronache/migranti-laustria-d-lavvio-ai-controlli-mirati-ai-confini-1429775.html (Visited 23 May 2020).

Schmitt, Carl. 1921. *Die Diktatur*. Bristol: Polity Press, 2013.

Scott, Mark. 2020. 'Social Media Giants Are Fighting Coronavirus Fake News. It's Still Spreading Like Wildfire', *Politico*, online edition, 12 March. www.politico.com/news/2020/03/12/social-media-giants-are-fighting-coronavirus-fake-news-its-still-spreading-like-wildfire-127038 (Visited 3 June 2020).

Law, rights, and public policy 79

Serhan, Yasmeen. 2020. 'The Case Against Waging "War" on the Coronavirus', *The Atlantic*, online edition, 31 March. www.theatlantic.com/international/archiv e/2020/03/war-metaphor-coronavirus/609049/ (Visited 20 May 2020).

Singh, Sonali. 2020. 'India's Response to Covid-19: A Softpower Perspective', *Center of Public Diplomacy, University of Southern California*, 15 May. www. uscpublicdiplomacy.org/blog/india%E2%80%99s-response-covid-19-soft-powe r-perspective (Visited 20 May 2020).

Sircar, Anisha. 2020. 'India's Coronavirus Lockdown is Bringing Out the Worst in its Police Force', *Quartz India*, online edition, 28 March. https://qz.com/ india/1826387/indias-coronavirus-lockdown-brings-police-brutality-to-the-fore/ (Visited 20 May 2020).

Sodha, Sonia. 2020. 'Nudge Theory Is a Poor Substitute for Hard Science in Matters of Life or Death', *The Guardian*, online edition, 26 April (Visited 20 May 2020).

Sonn, Jung Won. 2020. 'Coronavirus: South Korea's Success in Controlling Disease is Due to its Acceptance of Surveillance', 19 March. https://theconversation.c om/coronavirus-south-koreas-success-in-controlling-disease-is-due-to-its-accepta nce-of-surveillance-134068 (Visited 11 June 2020).

Steinbeis, Maximilian. 2020. 'Noch lange kein Polizeistaat', *Verfassunblog*. 'On Constitutional Matters'. 4 April. https://verfassungsblog.de/noch-lange-kein-po lizeistaat/ (Visited 20 May 2020).

Takahashi, Ikuo, Mayu Arimoto and Mariko Kurokawa. 2020. *New Coronavirus vs Privacy-Contact Tracing and Law*, Japanese edition. Amazon Kindle Publishing, loc. 2790, 2803, 2816, 2832, 2850.

Tanaka, Keiko. 1994) *Advertising Language: A Pragmatic Approach to Advertisements in Britain and Japan*. Abingdon: Routledge.

Tannen, Deborah. 2013. 'The Argument Culture', *Daedalus—American Democracy & the Common Good* Spring: 177. www.amacad.org/publication/argument-cult ure (Visited 23 May 2020).

Tian, Yew Lun. 2020. 'In "People's War" on Coronavirus, Chinese Propaganda Faces Pushback', *Reuters World News*, 13 March. www.reuters.com/article/u s-health-coronavirus-china-propaganda-a/in-peoples-war-on-coronavirus-chine se-propaganda-faces-pushback-idUSKBN2100NA (Visited 20 May 2020).

United Kingdom Department of Health & Social Care. 2020. 'What the Coronavirus Bill Will Do', 26 March. www.gov.uk/government/publications/coronavirus-bil l-what-it-will-do/what-the-coronavirus-bill-will-do (Visited 23 May 2020).

Vitale, Alex. 2018. *The End of Policing*. New York: Verso Books.

Wacks, Raymond. 1984. 'Judges and Injustice', *South African Law Journal* 101: 266.

Wacks, Raymond. 1991. 'Judges and Moral Responsibility', in W. Sadurski (ed.), *Ethical Dimensions of Legal Theory, Poznan Studies in the Philosophy of the Sciences & the Humanities*, 111–129. Amsterdam: Rodopi.

Wacks, Raymond. 1998. 'Law's Umpire: Judges, Truth, and Moral Accountability', in Peter Koller and André-Jean Arnaud (eds.), *Law, Justice, and Culture*, 75–83, Stuttgart: Franz Steiner Verlag.

Wacks, Raymond. 2000. 'Are Judges Morally Accountable?', in *Raymond Wacks, Law, Morality, and the Private Domain*, pp. 91–111. Hong Kong: Hong Kong University Press.

Wacks, Raymond. 2009. 'Injustice in Robes: Iniquity and Judicial Accountability', *Ratio Juris* 22: 128.

80 *Law, rights, and public policy*

Wang, Jason, Chun Ng and Robert Brook. 2020. 'Response to COVID-19 in Taiwan. Big Data Analytics, New Technology, and Proactive Testing', *Journal of the American Medical Association* 323(14): 1341. doi:10.1001/jama.2020.3151.

Williams, Elliot. 2020. 'COVID-tracing framework privacy busted by bluetooth' hackaday.com/2020/09/03/covid-tracing-framework-privacy-busted-by-bluetooth/ (Visited 18 September 2020).

Wong, Tessa. 2020. 'Shincheonji and Coronavirus: The Mysterious "cult" Church Blamed for S Korea's Outbreak', *BBC News*, 14 March. www.bbc.com/news/av/world-asia-51851250/shincheonji-and-coronavirus-the-mysterious-cult-church-blamed-for-s-korea-s-outbreak (Visited 1 June 2020).

Yglesias, Matthew. 2020. 'The End of Policing Left me Convinced We Still Need Policing', Vox, 18 June. www.vox.com/2020/6/18/21293784/alex-vitale-end-of-policing-review (Visited 22 July 2020).

4 The technology of information

> The security of power is built upon the insecurity of the citizen.
> Leonardo Sciascia, *The Knight and Death*[1]

Power rests in the hands of those who control the production and managing of the technology we use and, in particular, the technology of information. Information is power, but it is also true that whoever owns the technology that produces data, controls information. When we mention the 'technology of information' we do not refer to 'computer' or 'information' technology. These pertain to the building of tools to allow the management of data and not to the manner in which data are managed. In other words, there is a difference between the architect who designs a house and the masons who build it: the masons may—of course—be highly skilled, but they are not architects. What often happens, however, is that the 'mere' fact of being a competent computer expert (whether a programmer or a 'data scientist') allows such a person to claim expertise in disciplines such as law and economics 'just' because the so-called experts are tasked to build the tools to implement the next technology of information or, in brief, to 'implement the algorithm'. The PGP case discussed below involved a programmer of encryption software who was neither a cryptologist nor a security expert. Data scientists facilitate the acquisition of knowledge, they do not create it.

This widespread misconception is captured by the Greek artist, Apelles of Kos, who warned a shoemaker who claimed he could teach him how to create his art: *Ne supra crepidam, sutor!* Similarly, it is not for a computer expert to say *what* data are relevant to research, *how* these data should be matched, and *what* the results mean because that is the domain of the researcher. In other words, if you need someone to develop a platform to calculate the motion of molecules under the kinetic theory of gases you best employ a physicist who understands how to use Python programming language rather than a computer expert that has (if any) some grasp of physics. The latter may come in handy to review the source code or the design of

---

1 Sciascia, Leonardo. *Il cavaliere e la morte* (Gli Adelphi) (p. 32). Quotation translated by Andrea Monti.

82 *The technology of information*

the software, but albeit important, this is merely a secondary role. However obvious this point may appear, too frequently it is overlooked. Moreover, on a larger scale the same problem arises in respect of the development of complex infrastructures to process large amounts of data.

Similar considerations apply to the management of public safety and security during a pandemic. Science has, of course, been important in understanding the nature of the Coronavirus and the pursuit of a vaccine and therapy. Nevertheless it has not contributed significantly to innovation in the control and eradication of the virus. This is because the measures adopted, contact tracing and quarantine, are the very same measures that were employed in the past. It was technology at large—and in particular, the cultural approach toward the legal issues relating to technology in the management of information that made the difference in regard to the effectiveness of the response to the pandemic. From contact tracing to mapping the availability of protective masks, from geo-fencing to monitoring, the public policy options relied upon the exclusive will of those who de facto control the *technology of information*. Complex algorithms, training datasets, software implementation, and computing power are beyond the reach of public authorities. Thus the more this technology is in the hands of the private sector, the fewer the options of policymakers and less independent they are to pursue them, and vice versa.

'Exposure notification' is a paradigmatic case—although not the only one—that explains the concept in general terms. On the one hand, exposure notification has been widely possible only because Apple and Google decided to modify the operating system that makes smartphones work to make Bluetooth features available to programmers. On the other hand, by worshipping the cult of privacy, many EU countries rejected the opportunity to use the embedded geolocation features to enhance the effectiveness of exposure notification. In view of the connection between technology, power, and fundamental rights the pandemic exposed another recognized but underestimated question: who is the collector of the deluge of data generated by the pandemic, and who is able to interpret these data and understand the result of the analysis?

As discussed in Chapter 2, data have been an essential part of determining the outcome of government policies: the more reliable the data, the more effective the decisions and, of course, the less reliable, the more ineffective these policies have been. The ramifications of these issues are broad and intricate, and extend well beyond specific technical aspects. They raise the matter of who (or what) actually governs a country and how. In the West, the relationship between technology of information, on the one hand, and industry and power, on the other, has been affected by a change in the economic and political strategies that fostered the building of a consent-manufacturing rule, but also by a cultural rejection of a comprehensive digital transformation based on the obsession with surveillance that, regrettably, slowed down the response to the pandemic.

The genesis of mass surveillance

The fixation in Europe and the United States with the incubus of 'global surveillance' has created an overreaction to anything that resembles the collection of a mass of information by either the public or private sector. In respect of the latter, major tech firms and a myriad other business actors enticed us into believing that they could profit from 'profiling' their customers or by anonymous users accessing their websites or social media pages. This Western obsession is not, however, entirely without merit. In the 19th and 20th centuries several countries—of various political orientations—founded or enhanced their police and internal security systems, establishing a systematic collection of information about the citizen, to be retrieved on demand when required:

> The archetype of a politically oriented filing-system is the one established in Italy in 1894, when the circular n. 5116 of 25 May 1894 issued by the Directorate General of Public Security, established an office with the task of building and systematic updating the list of political opponents. Anarchists, republicans, socialists but also idlers and vagrants were the subject of a widespread surveillance activity that fed a substantial archive of personal files ... During the Fascist period, the surveillance and control activity of the police was expanded up to include not only the politicians, but a whole indeterminate category of people, defined as generically anti-fascist, and the Allogeni, that is, the ethnic minorities mainly settled in the region of Venezia Giulia.[2]

Police fingerprint archives and *Bertillonage*—the early (unsuccessful[3]) French attempt to create an anthropometric database—have been used since the beginning of the 1900s to identify suspects, and in 1920 the US Federal Bureau of Investigation built the first fingerprint filing-system. Throughout Europe, including Russia, and irrespective of the imperial, monarchic, or democratic regimes, all shared a fear of possible mass revolution fuelled by Marxist and anarchist theories as well as by independentism. As a consequence, every State began establishing its own internal surveillance police, whose target was the political activism of those who threatened 'public order' and the 'morality' of their institutions. That was the objective, for example, of the 1936 British Public Order Act which was designed to address the threat posed to public order by fascist political activists. On the other hand, the Italian Fascist Royal Decree n. 31 of 1923 had the sole purpose of targeting socialists and Bolsheviks who were perceived to be a danger to public order. Techniques to preserve political power are clearly unrelated to political ideology.

---

2 Monti & Wacks 2019: 37.
3 Fosdik 1915–1916.

84 *The technology of information*

Mere surveillance as such, however, is no guarantee of success in defending the survival of the State, as illustrated by the failure of Третье отделение Собственной Его Императорского Величества канцелярии, the Tsarist political police known as 'the Third Section', to eradicate the new political ideas spreading around the country culminating in the 1905 October Revolution:

> The Revolution introduced into Russia a new pattern of politics common in the West , but completely alien and largely incomprehensible to tsardom's forces of order. The political police found itself in the forefront of an internal war, in a sense a civil war where its ethos, 'reaffirm the monarchical principle when it weakened , defend it when it was attacked', proved totally inadequate in the face of the tidal wave of violence and alien political concepts weeping over the nation.[4]

During WWII US authorities used the data from the Census Bureau to track and detain in internment camps Japanese and residents of Japanese descent,[5] while the Nazi regime resorted to IBM to obtain an electromechanical machine used to 'efficiently manage' the search for and deportation of Jews.[6] The East German *Staatssicherheitsdienst* administered a huge card-based filing system and later established a database of personal odours to be fed to specially trained dogs:

> The Ministry for State Security (Stasi) routinized the approach, building up a massive archive of people's smells. Started in 1979, the collection was kept across East Germany, collected and evaluated by the Main Department XX, responsible for monitoring the East German cultural and media scene and the repression of the political opposition.[7]

It may justly be claimed that 'the age of technology-powered surveillance' began West and East of the Iron Curtain long before the advent of computers and the Internet, and continued almost uninterrupted up to today as shown by post-Cold War scandals exposed by investigative journalists (*Echelon*, exposed in 1982 by James Bamford[8] and more exhaustively six years later by Duncan Campbell[9]) and by whistle-blowers (*Prism*,

---

4 Zuckermann 1992: 281.
5 Aratani 2018.
6 Black 2012: 56.
7 *Deutsches Spionagemuseum* 'Odour Capture'. www.deutsches-spionagemuseum.de/en/sammlung/odour-capture (Visited 13 June 2020).
8 Bamford 1983.
9 Campbell 1988.

The technology of information   85

unmasked by former US Central Intelligence Agency employee, Edward Snowden).[10]

Private profiling

In parallel, from the beginning of the 20th century the Western world was invaded by another form of surveillance fostered by a more mundane ideology—profit—rather than by 'doing the right thing' or *Realpolitik*. It is almost certainly the case that the most comprehensive mass surveillance programme in peacetime that used technologies of information and the computer revolution has been the creditworthiness and insurance private infrastructures. The initial approach was based on raw data: did the subject go bankrupt? Did he fail to honour his cheques? Did she have any civil judgements against her or any criminal convictions? The industry that offered credit protection then moved to creditworthiness checks relying upon analytics-based assessments and early warning activities rather than upon 'bare' facts. This translates, in the daily course of operation, into a 'score' that determines whether the individual is a safe risk to award him or her a loan, mortgage, or credit card. This highly invasive process delves into the personal lifestyle and individual preferences of millions of people. It is these companies, and not their contractual counterparts, that decide whether a deal can be struck or a home purchased. And these important decisions are made in the context of a fundamentally unequal relationship because from the selection of data to be collected to the criteria by which they are measured, the system is designed in favour of the creditor. Western economies might not impose the creditworthiness surveillance at the levels of the Chinese social scoring;[11] nonetheless they profoundly affect the lives of many individuals.

Bias by design is a major problem when the decision is (covertly) deferred to an automated process. And this is so despite the meticulously drafted statements about 'analytics services' that describe supporting the decisional process rather than leaving the decision *tout court* to an automated process. However disquieting this process is, it is small fry compared with the decisions affecting life and death situations such as criminal investigations. Similar, if not even more egregious, consequences occur in respect of the controlling of a health emergency as will become clear below.

Despite occasional complaints, however, no one actually challenges the value of these systems themselves, and the real power they wield. In the EU, for instance, notwithstanding the GDPR, no creditworthiness algorithm has so far been disclosed, and the actual logic of these analytics services is largely unknown outside the circles of the *cognoscenti*. Still, much of this

10 Kelion 2013.
11 Kobie 2019.

86 *The technology of information*

information is hidden in plain sight: they are just too complex to understand without a deep knowledge in various fields, from actuarial mathematics to database design, from psychometrics to logistics. This is a major problem because the actual decision is in the hands of those who control the technology of information that is the basis of the adoption of public policy. It is rarely possible for a policymaker to design, without technical assistance, the big policy picture, and there is a genuine risk that the 'support' of a policy choice shifts from accountable human 'experts' to faceless algorithms, thereby diluting political and legal accountability while those who control the data covertly make decisions that are not necessarily in the public interest.

Credit scoring surveillance was not simply a product of the public interest in a regular flow of economic transactions. Another major factor was the turning of the citizen into a spending machine, a process recently accelerated by the 'e-commerce revolution'. Crudely stated, capitalism—or more accurately, the free market—is based on transforming humans into febrile consumers of goods, driving them into debt regardless of their actual needs. To sustain itself, a market economy obviously requires its products to be sold, and this needs buyers to be induced or compelled into buying. Indeed, since the beginning of the 20th century these needs fuelled empirical and theoretical research to predict and influence human purchasing behaviour.

Public order management has long relied upon technology to control (and normalize) citizens' behaviour so that, aside from propaganda, there was no need to invest in the construction of individual 'behavioural profiles'. All that mattered was knowledge of 'everything' about 'everybody': who do you know, where you go, where you meet with whom, and what do you believe in, etc. By contrast, sales-oriented consent manufacturers and politicians' campaigners developed a no-holds-barred attitude to use theories of various types to understand and orient human behaviour toward their preferred outcomes, be it the sale of a car or the election of a President. What do the 1958 Ford Edsel Fiasco[12] and the 1934 American Institute of Public Opinion's successful forecast of Roosevelt as the next US President have in common despite the contrary prediction by the (until then) 'infallible' *Literary Digest*?[13]

The extraordinary series of mistakes and erroneous assumptions that doomed to failure Ford's new model of the late 1950s included resorting to 'motivational research':

> [Henry Ford's] main prophet was an Austrian professor named Ernest Dichter. He claimed that using psychoanalysis he could identify the 'deep motivations' of consumers and thus determine the positioning

---

12 Shah 2017.
13 Squire 1988.

The technology of information   87

of a product and direct its communication ... Ernest Dichter and his school produced resounding disasters. The most famous is the Ford Edsel fiasco (1958–1960) which was launched according to Dichter's theory that a car is a sexual (male) metaphor and failed miserably on the market. After a few episodes of this kind the bizarre professor lost all credibility in the United States. There were directives circulating in the most important multinational corporations warning against the use of such techniques.[14]

Freudian psychoanalysis and its various iterations have not, of course, been the sole approach to satisfying the desire to predict and influence human behaviour; the impact of Skinner's behaviourism and Jungian theory continue to this day, supported by the colossal amount of personal information and data available online, a matter we return to below. Nevertheless the problem remains the same: predictive models rarely work as promised.

In 1934, some twenty years before the shipwreck of the Edsel project, a then small US polling institute (later to become known as Gallup) sank the *Literary Digest* battleship in the clash to forecast the winner of the presidential election.[15] In a 'statistics vs Big Data' *ante litteram* contest, Gallup's pollster demonstrated how a minor, well- designed statistical sample of 50,000 subjects was superior to the ten million subscribers upon which the *Literary Digest* based its conclusions. Also, the irony should not pass unnoticed that the *Digest*'s approach was identical to that followed by many professional media and government advisers in managing the records of infections during the Coronavirus pandemic. What links the Edsel and the *Literary Digest* fiascos is *bias*. It is also notable that Gallup committed a similar mistake, failing to predict the winner of the 1948 US presidential election. As mentioned above, motivational research was biased in believing that the car is a male sexual metaphor:

> In the 1950s, there was a view among a certain section of experts that 'Motivational Research' was done with the pre-defined notion of 'sex' appeal ... Research done with preconceived notions will produce biased results.[16]

The *Literary Digest* failed because of a double bias: it based its prediction on a (relatively) small number of responses, neglecting the relevance of the non-received responses, or to consider that the readers of the magazine belonged to a particular social stratum that was not truly representative. The 1948 Gallup failure was the result of a different bias: creating a

14 Livraghi 1968.
15 Ohmer 2006.
16 Sheah 2020.

88 *The technology of information*

statistically valid sample requires selecting respondents by setting a series of criteria, but it is always possible—as happened to Gallup—to miss or wrongly assess a criterion relevant to understanding how people are likely to vote. In these cases what miscarried was the *technology* of information, or *the conceptual design of how relevant information should be identified, collected, organized, and processed.*

The findings of US applied psychology research crossed the Pacific and landed in the UK in the seventies. It occurred because of the change in the approach of industry and politicians toward customers and electors. The economic crisis forced businessmen and policymakers to find a different method by which to engage their 'constituencies' and move from an elitist and paternalistic approach toward the exploitation of the psychological motives driving a purchase:

> The advertising industry started to bring in Americans to run focus groups with British housewives. The consumers were encouraged to play at being products from household cleaners to car seatbelts. The aim was not to talk rational, but to act out and reveal the inner emotional relationship to products. And then a politician emerged who also believed that people should be allowed to express themselves. Instead of being controlled by the state the individual should become the central focus of society.[17]

The political dimension of this new approach is exemplified by the speech of Margaret Thatcher at the 1975 Conservative Party Conference as reported by Adam Curtis:

> Some Socialists seem to believe that people should be numbers in a State computer. We believe they should be individuals. We are all unequal. No one, thank heavens, is like anyone else, however much the Socialists may pretend otherwise. We believe that everyone has the right to be unequal but to us every human being is equally important …
>
> A man's right to work as he will, to spend what he earns, to own property, to have the state as servant and not as master, they are the essence of a free economy. On that freedom all our other freedoms depend.[18]

A paradoxical consequence of this appeal to individualism is that the consumer (and the voter) would lose his or her independent judgement:

---

17 Curtis 2002b.
18 Thatcher, Margaret. 1975. Speech to Conservative Party Conference. Winter Gardens, Blackpool. www.margaretthatcher.org/document/102777 (Visited 15 June 2020).

The technology of information 89

emphasizing discrete differences facilitated the herding of the electorate—a situation that would have been exacerbated by the 'computer revolution'.

The computer revolution in surveillance and control

In the early years of the digital revolution, computers and computing were widely used in advanced countries, principally the United States. This occurred in various sectors: scientific research, telecommunication, insurance, finance, and banking, and, of course, government. The *fil rouge* that connected these quite disparate domains and the many others where the digital transformation began is the method by which data were entered into the system: a manual input of fixed sets of data, mainly collected by analogue supports. Individuals were shielded from private and public intrusions because the technology of the time did not allow a direct collection of data pertaining to a subject, so a proxy was necessary in the shape of a form, an application, or whatever else worked as 'storage' whose content was to be reversed in the computer.

Change began in the 1980s when computer networks became widely available to private individuals in the form of electronic bulletin boards, and then, in the early 1990s, as Internet-connected resources. This was the moment when, for the first time, information relating to individuals was generated *natively* in a digitized form by these individuals themselves, and by way of a machine-to-machine exchange of data. And this was also the moment when a (relatively) small number of people began to ask themselves questions about the impact of this technology on fundamental rights.

A rich bibliography flourished in this period, accounting for the birth of the hacking movement in the United States[19,20] and Europe,[21] the criminal[22,23,24] and the digital underground, and the early development of the core concepts of the pro-privacy and anti-techno-surveillance culture[25] as well as of the free-software and open source movements.[26] It is not our purpose to provide a comprehensive history of the role of hacking in shaping the world as we know and experience it today. Suffice it to say, in contrast to received wisdom, hacking culture played a fundamental role in the development of the digital industry and in the setting of the legal and political

---

19 Levy 1984.
20 Sterling 1992.
21 Chiccarelli & Monti 1997, 2011.
22 Mungo & Clough 1993.
23 Stoll 1989.
24 Hafner & Markoff 1995.
25 Ludlow 1996.
26 Raymond 1999.

90 *The technology of information*

agenda in many countries. An important, controversial, and relevant example is the PGP case.[27]

In a nutshell it contains almost all the elements for reconsidering the relationship between public (or national) security and individual rights. In 1991 an American computer scientist, Phil Zimmermann, created a self-explanatory computer programme called 'Pretty Good Privacy' or 'PGP'. For some time it offered 'strong encryption' thanks to the application of public-key cryptography, a technology of information by which to share confidential messages over an insecure channel, described in 1976 by Whitfield Diffie and Martin Hellman[28] and later independently engineered in 1978,[29] as an algorithm called 'RSA' after the names of its inventors, Ron Rivest, Adi Shamir, and Leonard Adleman from the Massachusetts Institute of Technology. Zimmermann, who neither invented public-key cryptography nor the RSA algorithm that played an important role in the computer security, had the means to transform them into a usable computer programme that, for the first time, allowed *everybody* to experience a very high level of protection even against the mighty US government.

Until PGP remained within US borders nothing happened, but when the software was made available through an FTP server (a computer protocol that allows file exchange) to the rest of the world the situation abruptly changed. The US government opened an investigation into a suspected infringement of the weapon export control legislation that prohibited the export of strong encryption because of its legal correspondence with actual weapons. Zimmermann reacted by publishing the programme's source code (the blueprint that allows anyone to rebuild it) in a book[30] whose content was designed to be returned to its pristine digital form by scanning or re-typing. Computer programmes, he said, may well be subjected to export control as such, but books containing the source code are protected by the US Constitution's First Amendment free speech provision. This argument was later affirmed by the US Court of Appeals for the Ninth Circuit.[31] For various reasons, including the release of the encryption export control's regulations, the Zimmermann case was never pursued and the federal investigation was dropped. There are, however, several aspects of the episode that are worth mentioning.

First, PGP demonstrates the actual value (or danger) of the option to self-engineer a technology of information for political purposes: Zimmermann's

---

27 Garfinkel 1994.
28 Diffie & Hellman 1976: 644–654.
29 Rivest, Shamir, & Adleman 1978.
30 Zimmermann 1995.
31 US Court of Appeals for the Ninth Circuit. 1999. *BERNSTEIN V USDOJ Case Number: 97-16686.* www.ce9.uscourts.gov/web/newopinions.nsf/f606ac175e010d64882566eb 00658118/febd2452a8a4d79b8825676900685b71?OpenDocument (Visited 13 June 2020).

The technology of information   91

privacy concerns were, in fact, largely related to government surveillance activities rather than to an as yet non-existent private industry based on profiling. Second, notwithstanding their efforts, the US government did not succeed in preventing PGP from leaking outside the United States and into European servers either via digital upload or book shipping. Even the paramount interest in national security could not easily outweigh technology-assisted free-speech protection. Third, freedom of speech has been instrumental in protecting the right to privacy. Without the First Amendment to safeguard the right to print a computer programme's source code as a book, the right to privacy would have lost a vital practical tool. Fourth, and most importantly, PGP was perhaps the first case where a *concern*—not an actual threat—led to the enforcement of a *precaution principle* based on a substantial lack of trust (again, not without merit) toward the government. This was the foundation of the mainstream legal approach to an almost religious attitude toward privacy and other fundamental rights that are invoked as unassailable shields against any governmental activity. Actually, human-rights-as-a-shield is in any event a questionable position as these rights are routinely weighed against other competing interests of the State by the judiciary.

Information technology and a panopticon society

Forceful arguments concerning the tension between individual privacy and the activities of the State continue to characterize academic and activist debates. In fact, however, the computer industry felt no need to participate in this discourse. It was only many years later—when 'security' meant 'business' that their commercial ears pricked up. The creation of the Internet 'for the rest of us'—to paraphrase the famous Apple advertisements—revealed little concern for the intrinsic deficiencies of the Internet Protocol version IV (Ipv4). Designed for the academic world—where mutual trust was taken for granted—this 'digital Esperanto' that permits a computer 'speaking' different 'languages' to exchange information is unsafe. Over time, but at the cost of accidents, data losses, and criminal acts, layers of security have been added and it is a telling coincidence that the spreading of computer viruses exhibited striking similarities with a pandemic. Initially, when computers were mainly isolated because of the lack of a network connection, the contagion happened by way of floppy disks. Incidentally, it is a triple irony that one of very first mass computer-virus infections was caused in 1989 by an anthropologist working as a consultant for the World Health Organization that distributed thousands of infected floppy disks apparently meant to provide information about the AIDS virus.[32]

---

32 Edgar 2002: 215.

92 *The technology of information*

The contagion was slow as the infected means of data storage had to physically travel from one PC to another and it was easier to adopt digital hygiene policies such as the advice not to not use unknown memory supports (do not share drink or food), always run the antivirus before inserting somebody else's floppy disk into the drive of your computer (sanitize tools before use), set your memory support to 'read-only' mode when using somebody else's computer (wear a protective mask). The spread of viruses accelerated, and became almost undetectable when, via the Internet, computers were directly accessible by malware, ransomware, and other pernicious software. Moreover, the operative speed needs of the 'information society'—where email messages have to be answered before they are even sent and tasks fulfilled at the very moment they are assigned—were met by people not well versed in the use of computers (the majority of humans!) that downplayed the importance of proper security-oriented behaviour. Like the pandemic-deniers, the fatalists, or the 'irresponsibles' who continue recklessly to defy the Coronavirus guidelines, these computer operators enhanced the spreading of malware by clicking on the wrong email attachment, visiting infected websites, and bypassing the rules imposed by their security manager.

Finally, in the same way as biological viruses overpower the immune system and are more successful against weak hosts, a computer virus spreads by exploiting the intrinsic vulnerabilities of an operating system (the 'core' computer programme that allows an operator to interact with the machine in order to obtain the desired output). The main difference between the two conditions, however, is that the victim of a biological virus has some, albeit limited, responsibility for the weakness of his or her immune system, whereas a computer operating system is designed from scratch and, as such, should be made with appropriate sturdiness. Of course, it is not possible to create a flawless computer programme, but that does not imply that designers should be free to ignore, or diminish the importance of this requirement.

The root of the problem—lack of security-oriented design and lack of users' awareness—remains in place, and it has eased the creation of the dreaded—yet questionable—notion of 'surveillance capitalism'.[33] This widely acclaimed analysis fails to capture the real problem which is that of

---

33 Zuboff 2019. She defines this phenomenon as '1. A new economic order that claims human experience as free raw material for hidden commercial practices of extraction, prediction, and sales; 2. A parasitic economic logic in which the production of goods and services is subordinated to a new global architecture of behavioral modification; 3. A rogue mutation of capitalism marked by concentrations of wealth, knowledge, and power unprecedented in human history; 4. The foundational framework of a surveillance economy; 5. As significant a threat to human nature in the twenty-first century as industrial capitalism was to the natural world in the nineteenth and twentieth; 6. The origin of a new instrumentarian power that asserts dominance over society and presents startling challenges to market democracy; 7. A movement that aims to impose a new collective order based on total certainty; 8. An expropriation of critical human rights that is best understood as a coup from above: an overthrow of the people's sovereignty'.

The technology of information   93

manipulative control. It is not surveillance as much as the control exercised through nudging, psychometrics etc that is at the heart of the market of personal data for commercial or political gain.

The expansion of Internet-based business has not been accompanied by the development of an increased awareness between users and the services they are offered, mainly 'for free' (as in 'free beer' not as in 'freedom', as Richard Stallman points out).[34] In other words, the hacking community, once almost a lost civilization, became yet more isolated from the rest of the world that displayed no interest in the matter of digital rights. Users just want to enjoy a video, or let the world know that they exist by making public frivolous or trivial information about their whereabouts without the slightest concern whether these facts are being collected and processed. The insouciance of the overwhelming majority of social network users with regard to the protection of their intimate selves speaks volumes.

The growth of the technology of information

This indifference enhanced the evolution of the sectors of industry based on the collection and analysis of data and personal information available online. It was not only the omnipresent Big Tech firms that exploited this willingness of individuals to expose their private lives. Others such as insurance companies, banks, and financial institutions that were already accustomed to dealing with huge amounts of information were attracted to the prospect of complementing their databases with other, more direct, and personalized information about their own customers. They developed sophisticated technologies of information to calculate the 'insurability' or the creditworthiness of an individual and, in general, the cost of uncertainty.

In the course of time, therefore, the need for data-gathering policing begins to converge with those of the private sector which has become a repository of a wealth of information of interest to the police and security agencies. And while these bodies could only expand their collection of raw data by way of interception at various levels, the private sector had gained access to the *minds* of the people, permanently stored in huge data centres. In fact, a government or a State lost its unique control over the ocean of information generated every millisecond by the terminals connected to the network. By contrast—and unless it adopted undemocratic means—it could never dream of collecting so much information about its citizens as the Big Tech firms do. Should a Western country announce the creation of a State-administered social network or a State-operated search engine more than an eyebrow of perplexity would be raised and 'mass surveillance paranoia' would skyrocket!

Strangely enough, and despite all the disquiet surrounding the manifold threats to privacy online, individuals are more willing to trust their personal

---

34 Williams 2002.

94 *The technology of information*

data to private companies than to public institutions. From the perspective of governments, though, what matters is that all information is there and made available by the tech giants (including Internet and telecom operators) 'on call' whether it is to protect 'national security' or the health of citizens. This is a rapidly expanding pattern which started with the discreet formation of mandatory data retention of Internet traffic data, and enlarged to include various methods to access information held by private companies.

Recalling a 2014 conversation in the London quarters of Palantir (the US company that during the pandemic signed a deal with the British government to access citizens' data for a pandemic-related project, discussed below), Cambridge Analytica whistle-blower, Cristopher Wylie writes:

> [I]t was pointed out that government security agencies, along with contractors like Palantir, couldn't legally mass-harvest personal data on American citizens, but—here's the catch—polling companies, social networks and private companies could. And despite the ban on directly surveilling Americans, I was told that US intelligence agencies were nonetheless able to make use of information on American citizens that was 'freely volunteered' by US individuals or companies.[35]

There is, though, more than one point of contact between what the masters of the (alleged) 'surveillance capitalism' promise to do and what governments intend to achieve by phishing in the sea of personal information gathered by the private sector. There is a growing interest in 'predictive' technologies and automated 'AI-powered' analysis to detect 'radicalization' or other potentially criminal acts. Governments, nonetheless, share with 'surveillance capitalists' another goal:

> [To] acquire ever-more-predictive sources of behavioral surplus: our voices, personalities, and emotions. Eventually, surveillance capitalists discovered that the most-predictive behavioral data come from intervening in the state of play in order to nudge, coax, tune, and herd behavior toward profitable outcomes. Competitive pressures produced this shift, in which automated machine processes not only know our behavior but also shape our behavior at scale.[36]

In regard to public policy, this is a transition from a 19th century 'raw' form of fact-based surveillance (knowing who did what, when, where, how, and with whom) into a 20th century psychologically grounded manipulation of

---

35 Wylie 2019: Kindle Location 1826. For the record, Palantir stated that its employee contacted Cambridge Analytica in his personal capacity. 'Confessore, Nicholas, Rosenberg, Matthey "Spy Contractor's Idea Helped Cambridge Analytica Harvest Facebook Data"', *New York Times* 27 March 2018. www.nytimes.com/2018/03/27/us/cambridge-analytica-palantir.html (Visited 17 June 2020).
36 Zuboff 2019: 8.

The technology of information   95

the citizen, and a 21st century automated influencing tool based on 'personality traits'. Before analyzing the impact of these technologies of information, we need to ask whether these 'behavioural' or 'personality' analyses actually work. The answer is relevant to understanding the relationship between the decisions based on the need to control a pandemic and the restriction of civil liberties. This requires a brief explanation of a number of key matters.

The technology of profiling

There are five fundamental factors. First, it is important to recognize the distinction between 'understanding', 'influencing', and 'predicting'. 'Understanding' human behaviour (in its broadest sense) is the central preoccupation of psychology. This leads to 'influencing' which may be achieved through the application of various 'doctrines'—from Jungian to behaviourism or cognitivism—to treat mental disorders. 'Predicting' is functional to the attempt to solve non-psychiatric mental illness. The approaches of each branch of psychology may differ, but all are based on observation and some form of classification; in other words, 'profiling'.

A second critical factor is that, regardless of the specific approach, the tell-tale signs for both analysis and therapy arise out of a variety of epiphenomena: demeanour, body language, tics, voice tone, speech (in)capability, logical (dis)function, micro expressions, and so on. The only limit to these signs is the prospect of detecting them; thus the more sophisticated the methods available to identify these phenomena, the greater number of signs that are available to the psychologist. It is no surprise in this context that there is a growing interest in neurosciences to associate external reactions to specific parts of the brain, and to genetics to link behaviour to the presence (or absence) of specific genes. Third, the spreading of interactive, computer-based technologies offers the psychologist access to a whole range of new signs formerly unavailable or undetectable. Fourth, evolution of statistics and mathematics, new programming languages, computing resources, and the capability to gather information from a huge quantity of sources render it possible to undertake an entirely different, though not necessarily better, kind of analysis.

Finally, and this is crucial, at the heart of contemporary psychology is the ability to discover a much wider variety of signs rather than simply their quantity. On the other hand, politicians, and, more recently, industry, have succeeded or failed because of their capacity to 'read' and influence people. The more powerful the instruments to control the masses, the more the _status quo_—or profits—are guaranteed, hence the interest in the practical application of psychology's findings about human behaviour. This is precisely what occurred in the early 20th century in the United States with the implementation of Edward Bernays' syncretic approach based on

96 *The technology of information*

Freud's psychoanalysis and Le Bon's psychology of the masses.[37] The 1960s witnessed the emergence of the 'Me Generation' spawned in part by the theories of the (former Freudian) Wilhelm Reich. It is no exaggeration to say that this development transformed Americans and eventually the whole of Western society into mass consumers.[38]

In other words, there is nothing novel or surprising in the techniques deployed by modern-day 'surveillance capitalists'. Their methods and objectives attracted criticism in seminal works such as Vance Packard's *The Hidden Persuaders*[39] and, ironically by those published by Edward Bernays himself, including *Crystallizing Public Opinion*[40] and *Propaganda*.[41] The simple reality is that long before the advent of the Internet and the wicked manipulators of personal choice, vast amounts of personal information were collected and still are. Industry engaged in the design of new products and services to facilitate the collection of users' data. 'Analytics tools' were made available even to family businesses and owners of websites. And countless government bodies, researchers, advertising agencies, and others increasingly rely on these data to achieve their objectives.

Light-years separate the Gallup-*Literary Digest* quest to divine the next US President and the sophisticated techniques applied by Barack Obama's campaign.[42] Nonetheless we should not underestimate the effectiveness of 'micro-targeting', behavioural analysis, big data, and all the paraphernalia adopted during a political campaign to achieve their purpose. The similarity of the goals and attitude toward individuals manifested by advertising and politics—and, more recently, policing—is evident in the superimposition of the methods used to influence consumers and electors. 'Profiling' and 'psychometrics' are among the most popular techniques adapted from the advertising industry. In the words of the renowned copywriter, Rosser Reeves:

> One of the surprising things is how many of them believe that American advertising men are employing deep Freudian techniques. They believe that we are manipulating people, that we have sunk pipelines down to the pre-Oedipal wellsprings, that we are practicing some dark, mysterious necromancy ... As all top advertising men know, such talk is the sheerest nonsense ... it may pick up, along the way, people who are prone to believe in the sensational; but there are no hidden persuaders.

---

37 Le Bon 1895.
38 Curtis 2020.
39 Packard 1957.
40 Bernays 1923.
41 Bernays 1928. See too Nelson 2013.
42 Issenberg 2013.

The technology of information 97

Advertising works openly, in the bare and pitiless sunlight ... Good advertising men, like scientists, want research that is duplicable.[43]

Reeves expressed this view in 1961 and his book is manifestly out-of-date in several respects. Nevertheless, his assessment of the role of 'profiling' remains piquant. The methodology has, of course, improved dramatically, especially the collection of users' data as part of the price of access to the various online services, but we still await proof of how 'deterministic' and effective these 'surveillance capitalism' predictive tools are. As Reeves puts it, 'an experiment that works one way today and another way tomorrow is very much like the drunk who is hanging on to a lamppost. He is depending on it less for illumination than support'.[44]

Practices such as neuro-linguistic programming are born and built to talk directly to our inner self, piercing the veil of social pretence by way of face-to-face manipulative techniques such as 'mirroring', 'lateral eye movement', and 'calibration'. But when we are online, unburdened by the weight of our physical body—or lulled into a false sense of anonymity because of our 'secret' profile—we allow ourselves to indulge in behaviour we would never undertake in the 'real' world:

This is in part because friends, colleagues, spouses and parents typically see only part of your life, where your behaviour is moderated by the context of that relationship. Your parents may never see how wild you can get at a 3 a.m. rave after dropping two hits of MDMA, and your friends may never see how reserved and deferential you are in the office with your boss all have slightly different impressions of who you are. But Facebook peers into your relationships, follows you around in your phone, and tracks what you click and buy on the internet. This is how data from the site becomes more reflective of who you 'really are' than the judgments of friends or family.[45]

The longstanding criticism of psychometry and similar techniques is essentially based, as already mentioned, on the lack of measurability—and therefore reproducibility—of the results. What social networking and, in general, the platforms that attract a sufficiently large number of followers have been able to provide, though, is the possibility of testing and verifying these theories if not in real time, speedily enough to adapt the model to the findings, and with a greater number of variables to improve it:

43 Reeves 1961.
44 Ibid, 56.
45 Wylie 2019: Kindle Location 1682.

98 *The technology of information*

Compared with the accuracy of various human judges reported in the meta-analysis (20), computer models need 10, 70, 150, and 300 Likes, respectively, to outperform an average work colleague, cohabitant or friend, family member, and spouse.[46]

Yet this does not lead ineluctably to the conclusion that the Five Factor Model (FFM) described above is capable of delivering deterministic results. Why not? First, because its theoretical assumption that we can 'collapse' all traits of the human behaviour into five categories has no universal value:

If the FFM is a human universal and represents a 'solid beginning for under-standing personality everywhere' (McCrae & Costa, 1997, p. 515), it should replicate everywhere and under a broad range of environments and populations. To date, the FFM has yet to be tested in an indigenous, preliterate society. The vast majority of samples from cross-cultural studies are often urban students, glibly referred to as western, educated, industrialized, rich, democratic (WEIRD) populations (Henrich, Heine, & Norenzayan, 2010). Despite the wide range of cultures and languages where the FFM has been tested, WEIRD populations might show a similar personality structure if trait covariance is an artefact of living in large urban, literate populations.[47]

Second, computer-based trait predictions are prone to hidden or unrecognized bias. The research is designed so that the personality-revealing clues that feed the algorithm are predetermined by the researchers. A subset of these hints trains the computer programme that makes the algorithm work, and another subset functions as a test: the software is fed with the suggestions and states the results which are compared with the training data. By using different personality pointers and algorithms it is possible to choose the most effective profiling elements, the proper algorithm, and its more reliable software implementation:

The disadvantages are that researchers have no means of explaining their findings empirically. Further, some computer algorithms can be 'black box', meaning that even the creators do not have full access to how their algorithms work. These methods are problematic because researchers understand the algorithm's inputs and outputs but not what happens internally. Consequently, researchers can be ignorant of

---

46 Youyou, Kosinski, & Stillwell 2015.
47 Gurven, von Rueden, Massenkoff, & Kaplan 2013.

The technology of information   99

hidden biases, and the algorithm becomes 'accountable' for taking particular courses of action.[48]

Does 'profiling' actually work? Of course the devotees of such technologies of information are highly effective in presenting evidence that information about individuals' interests, opinions, and beliefs matched with their personality traits provide the basis of an accurate and fitting direct marketing or political campaign. These claims must, however, be taken with more than a grain of salt until there is an adequate level of intersubjective verification to guarantee deterministic results. The problem is that followers of these methods (pretend to) forget that human beings have the ability to control their reactions. This means that if a personality trait-based algorithm exploits my weakness in order to sell me a product, feed me fake news, or spin a political message, my critical thinking is normally able to detect and defuse the attack. In the words of the adage attributed to Gandhi: 'I will not let anyone walk through my mind with their dirty feet'.

Of course, where the target is ignorant enough and prone to absorb whatever message is delivered without any critical filter, such systems will be effective, at least in the short term. But we should be slow to underestimate the consequences of a continual and massive exposure to tailored, subjective communications that might induce a permanent shift in opinion. In the end, though, notwithstanding all these apprehensions, the perception among policymakers and businessmen is that 'profiling works'.

An empirical check

Although large-scale analytics are widely used at many levels and in almost every sector, there is a paucity of evidence regarding its efficacy. The most celebrated examples are the Barack Obama presidential campaign, mentioned above, and the notorious Cambridge Analytica scandal. Early in 2018 it emerged that Cambridge Analytica (CA), 'a military contractor and psychological warfare firm',[49] was accused of attempting to influence the results of the 2016 US Presidential elections in favour of Donald Trump through the analysis of data from 87 million Facebook profiles and their subsequent exploitation in the form of tailored messages and hidden communications with US Facebook users. These profiles were acquired by another organization to which an East European researcher from the University of Cambridge belonged; he, in turn, obtained them thanks to a research agreement with Facebook.

The case is commonly regarded as a combination of invasion of privacy, data theft, and (attempted) election manipulation. But this is to

48 Hinds & Joinson 2019.
49 Wylie 2019: Kindle Location 59.

100 *The technology of information*

misunderstand what happened. There is no invasion of privacy when we voluntarily and knowingly disclose personal information.[50] In the absence of a confidential relationship in which one's confidant (lawyer, doctor) is under a legal duty to maintain confidentiality, there is generally no violation of the right to privacy. In other words: authorizing a stranger (such as a Cambridge researcher) to access a private profile indicates that one has agreed to reduce the level of confidentiality of the information concerned. Nor is there any data theft; data cannot be stolen. They can be unlawfully copied, they can be destroyed, but they cannot be stolen because theft requires physical appropriation. Third, as argued above, there is nothing new in seeking to influence an electoral result in a more or less hidden manner. It is called 'propaganda' and has always existed.[51]

In the CA scandal, by contrast, there is no evidence that CA was actually able to influence the election results in the United States or elsewhere. They might have tried—and perhaps even succeeded, but none of the various investigations launched by data protection authorities and similar bodies around the world revealed a shred of evidence to support the allegations. This conclusion is sustained by bearing in mind that the only charges related to Facebook and that all of the accusations were limited to a mere violation of data protection law by failing to obtain users' consent before sharing their data. There was no official action taken against CA for staging a *coup*, nor any complaint for undermining US national security or for treason. Nor was CA or any of its officers indicted for any criminal offences.

Those, especially in the media, who have misrepresented the position have contributed to the misconception that even without positive evidence, deterministic manipulation is possible. This is not to say that profiling is innocuous or that we should not be concerned about the continual, unrelenting harvesting of personal information to covertly sway or overtly formulate public policy. Quite the reverse; we should have the right to know which technology of information we are subjected to and how it works: what is the anthropological framework used to select the digital breadcrumbs fed to the profiling model, where and what is the bias, how does the outcome influence both political choices and public policy. Worse than an effective, profiling-enhanced political strategy is a profile-based political strategy founded upon partial assumptions, unreliable data, flawed algorithms, and poor software applications. To repeat, it is not information technology (a tool to manipulate data), but the technology of information (what can be done to and with information) that is critical.

---

50 For a detailed analysis of what constitutes 'personal information' and the failure of the conventional 'privacy' approach, see Wacks 1980, 1989, 2013, and Monti & Wacks 2019.

51 See the works of Bernays cited above. Consider also the accusations against Italian Senator Achille Lauro who, in the 1950s and 1960s, was suspected of having earned his seat by handing over one shoe to the voters before the vote, and the other when there was proof that, in the secrecy of the voting booth, 'the right thing' had been done.

The technology of information 101

We tend to forget that as consumers of computer systems we only have ourselves to blame for being exploited. As users we have considerable power literally at our fingertips. We can prevent ourselves being X-rayed. But this control is one that very few (apart from the lost civilization of hackers) exercise despite the available technological and political alternatives, from open-source operating systems[52] and applications, to civil rights-friendly search engines[53] and social networks platforms.[54]

Oddly enough, however, the 'surveillance obsession' remains the standard (though hardly new) standpoint of scholars, journalists, and regulators that fuels the anti-technology prejudice that has existed since the world 'discovered' computers and the Internet, and is accepted as a shibboleth upon which to develop research, policies, and law. Instead of 'surveillance', a more appropriate characteristic of the current situation is 'control' in the sense of 'orienting', 'manipulating', or 'nudging'. And it is curious that the criticism of the abuse of data allegedly committed by Big Tech is not accompanied by a similar disdain for the use of behavioural economic theories, such as nudging that almost certainly contributed to the UK government's tardiness in responding to the pandemic. Many lives were thereby lost.

Notwithstanding the previous analysis, the question about the actual effectiveness of personality-traits profiling might make little sense because even though (automated) profiling is ineffective, the fact that people 'believe' it works renders it doubly dangerous. Consider the remark of Louis de Wohl (the astrologist hired by MI5 during WWII to deduce what the stars were telling the Nazis): 'It is entirely irrelevant whether we ourselves regard astrological advice as valuable and scientific or as useless nonsense. All that matters is that Hitler follows its rules'.[55]

A case study

In order to gain an understanding of the technologies of information involved in personality traits-based profiling and in the role played by users' data it is helpful to examine a specific aspect of the management of the pandemic in the UK. This case transcends national borders and provides an interesting example of the complexity of the issues related to policy-by-data.

On 28 March 2020 the British Government announced its strategy to use various technologies 'for coordinating the response with secure, reliable, and timely data—in a way that protects the privacy of our citizens—in order

---

52 Linux, free BSD, and OpenBSD are but a few free operating systems that do not contain a hidden surveillance feature.
53 Startpage (startpage.com) is a zero-knowledge search engine that does not retain any information from users' queries.
54 WikiTribune Social (wt.social) is a profiling-free social networking platform launched by Wikipedia founder, Jimmy Wales.
55 Milmo 2020.

102 *The technology of information*

to make informed, effective decisions'.[56] The ambition of the programme was considerable as was the quantity and quality of information to be processed. According to the official statement:

> [T]he data brought into the back end datastore held by NHS England and NHS Improvement will largely be from existing data sources e.g. data already collected by NHS England and NHS Improvement, Public Health England and NHS Digital. All NHS data remains under NHS England and NHS Improvement control.

In respect of the private sector's involvement, five companies were selected. These were Microsoft to provide support to store the data sources in its data centres, Amazon Web Services (if the convoluted writing has been correctly interpreted) to be used to make the platforms work, Google to collect real-time information on hospitals' response, Palantir Technologies UK to enable 'disparate data to be integrated, cleaned, and harmonized in order to develop the single source of truth that will support decision-making', and, finally, Faculty to carry out

> the development and execution of the data response strategy. This includes developing dashboards, models and simulations to provide key central government decision-makers with a deeper level of information about the current and future coronavirus situation to help inform the response.

On 5 June 2020 the civil rights media organization *openDemocracy* announced that it had obtained a part of the agreement between the British Government and four high-tech companies (Microsoft, Google, Cambridge Analytica partner Palantir, and Faculty):

> The contracts show that companies involved in the NHS datastore project, including Faculty and Palantir, were originally granted intellectual property rights (including the creation of databases), and were allowed to train their models and profit off their unprecedented access to NHS data. Government lawyers have now claimed that a subsequent (undisclosed) amendment to the contract with Faculty has cured this problem, however they have not released the further contract.[57]

There was some contradiction between the 28 March 2020 statement about the data to remain under the sole control of the NHS and the need subsequently to amend the text of the contract. (Incidentally, the original

---

56 Gould, Joshi, & Tang 2020.
57 Fitzgerald & Crider 2020.

The technology of information   103

statement mentioned only governmental 'control' and not the 'ownership' of data.) A detailed list of the services provided by Palantir to the British government is mentioned but is not accessible. Nevertheless on page 37 of the 60-page agreement,[58] the 'Nature and Purposes of the Processing' section reads as follows:

The aim of the project is to create a data store which will be used to:

1. Track and predict the spread of COVID-19;
2. Model interventions including guidance for public & patients;
3. Optimise health & community resources.

Processing many & varied data sources is critical for achieving these aims.

The processing will primarily focus on data triangulation to support tracking, surveillance and reporting for COVID-19.

As COVID-19 is now a pandemic and to ensure that we are taking a data-led approach, there are key questions which will need to be answered:

1. How do we track the spread of COVID-19 and the impact of it?
2. How do we predict the spread of COVID-19 and the impact of it?
3. How do we understand the impact of interventions?
4. How do we optimise the use of resources across the Healthcare System?
5. How do we equip the public with the resources and tools they need, to help themselves? The above are the primary purposes for which the data will need to be processed.

Page 38 of the agreement lists the type of personal data provided by the British Government to Palantir. It is worth quoting at length:

(i) personal contact details (including name , personal email address , home address,

> home telephone numbers, emergency contact details); (ii) personal details (including gender, nationality, place of birth); (iii) work contact details (including work email address, work department, work telephone numbers. user IDs, work location details; (iv) employment details (including job title, job duties, manager/sponsor, working hours, employee number); (v) any other personal data that may be useful for the nature and purposes of processing contemplated under the Agreement; and/or (vi) login and usage information required for the provision of software and services. Further, the Supplier will process Sensitive Personal Data (e.g. racial or ethnic origin) provided by (or at the direction of the Buyer) where such access is lawful and

58 https://cdn-prod.opendemocracy.net/media/documents/Palantir_Agreements.pdf

104 *The technology of information*

> critical in the performance of its obligations under the Agreement and the data to be processed may consist of (where applicable): (i) racial or ethnic origin where this is legally required/permitted or where the employee and/or contractor has consented , e.g. to comply with equality and diversity requirements; (ii) political affiliations, religious or similar beliefs where this is legally required I permitted or where the employee and/or contractor has consented , e.g. to allow statutory time off for religious purposes; (iii) criminal offences, proceedings and sentences where this is legally required/permitted or where the employee and/or contractor has consented (e.g. to protect the safety and security of staff and customers, or for insurance purposes); (iv) physical or mental health condition where this is legally required/permitted or where the employee and/or contractor has consented (e.g. to allow statutory time off for sickness, or to enable appropriate pay/employment adjustments to be made) and/or other Sensitive Personal Data provided for under the SOW or the applicable DPIA.

Furthermore, as stated on the same page, the government is bound to provide Palantir with

1. pseudonymised personal data
2. aggregated data—although this will not constitute personal data (albeit with risk of re-identification in the absence of proper controls) the Buyer instructs the Supplier to comply with the following paragraphs of the Framework Agreement Schedule 4 in relation to this data: 4, 5, 12, 13.

It is not known whether the British agreement is similar to the contract won by Palantir in the United States to support health authorities in respect of COVID-19. A spokesperson for the US Department of Health and Human Services commenting on Palantir's support in building a data platform called 'HHS Protect Now' stated:

> We are using the data aggregated ... to paint a picture for the Task Force, and state and local leaders to show the impact of their strategic decisions ... For instance, if there are a number of cases concentrated at a hospital next to an airport and a mass transit stop, we can build a predictive model using a transmission chain to predict how quickly the disease will spread taking into account these factors.[59]

He added that civil service-owned data will be merged with private datasets to build 'the single source for testing data'.[60]

---

59 Banco & Ackerman 2020.
60 Ibid.

The technology of information   105

By contrast, the British agreement (at least that part that was disclosed) does not contain any provision about the merging of Palantir's data sets with those of the government, or about the use of NHS data to train Palantir's algorithms or the NHS-owned algorithm. Moreover, there is no indication whether, in the case of the former, Palantir's algorithm and its application will be made permanently available to the government and on what legal basis. A similar analysis of the contract signed with Faculty[61] shows (pages 7–8) that the various services, the company is bound to provide, include:

- Support and help improve the NHSX Innovative Data Analytics capacity and capability, providing training and resource where necessary
- Scope and design a procurement specification for the development of validation datasets Run discovery into the technical architecture required for a platform allowing for AI products/services to be easily deployed and surfaced within clinical workflows.
- Development of change management frameworks and service redesign for adoption of AI-covering national, regional, and local levels and in line with the four priority areas of the AI in Health and Care Award.
- Modelling and simulation: using data from across the healthcare system to model scenarios to better understand the impact of the spread of COVID-19 on healthcare resources.
- Health system dashboard: presenting carefully curated information about COVID-19, and its impact on the healthcare system, to support decision making in response to the escalating spread of COVID-19.

Among additional services, Faculty is bound to 'provide access to secure sandbox environments which are to be made available to organizations selected by the Buyer for the purpose of testing and validating algorithms, during the COVID-19 Pandemic Response'. Even if the legalistic language of the contract makes it difficult to comprehend what Faculty is supposed to do, it is a fair assumption that the NHS Data Analytics platform will access clinical data in the whole patient workflow management, retrieve data located across the whole country, use healthcare data to train a Faculty-developed algorithm, and (help to) decide how to manage healthcare resources.

Page 14 of the agreement provides a hint of Palantir's role. Faculty will team with the latter to build a Health System Dashboard whose purpose is 'to present the information generated by the data and analyses'. In other words, Palantir undertakes the data processing and Faculty handles the (no less important) interface layer allowing it to interact with the various bits of information. GDPR-related information (page 48) apparently names, as the

---

61 https://cdn-prod.opendemocracy.net/media/documents/Faculty_Agreement.pdf (Visited 18 June 2020).

106 *The technology of information*

type of personal data to be processed, only pseudonymized and aggregated data, but there are no suggestions about the difficulty of the de-anonymization of both. Furthermore, there is a general reference to unidentified 'Sensitive Personal Data' and, under the 'Categories of Data Subjects' a cryptic reference reveals that Faculty will be permitted to process 'data provided or made available to the Supplier in relation to the Agreement' and, finally, a broad, unsatisfactory (under GDPR requirements) line mentions 'members of the public' and 'patients'.

In addition, if there is no connection between this agreement and the non-redacted part of a different one signed earlier with Faculty, the company is required by the British government to perform:

1. Identification, exploration and setup of alternative data sources (e.g. social media, utility providers and telecom bills, credit rating agencies, etc.) as well as data provided by MHCLG for monitoring and forecasting
2. Application of data science and machine learning across data provided by MHCLG and alternative data sources
3. Development of interactive dashboards which summarise the above activities into an easily consumable interface to inform policymakers. (G-Cloud 11 Call-Off Contract (version 4)—Buyer Contractual Details, 2020).[62]

The contract with Google is fairly meagre: it provides only that Google

> is offering to provide support free of charge to assist [NHS/NHSX/PHE?] with its efforts to tackle COVID-19. Google is providing support purely as a service to the public during the COVID-19-related public health emergency, and not as a gift to any individual government official.[63]

Article 5 of the agreement specifies 'The parties acknowledge and agree that it is not their intention to collect, access, share, use or otherwise process any personal data' and that should the necessity arise in the future, they will discuss the matter. It is not clear, then, if Google's involvement in the project remains the one announced in the statement of 28 March or whether something has changed given the fact that the British government, after an initial rejection, decided to follow the Google/Apple exposure notification

---

62 UK Crown Commercial Service. 9 April 2020. 'G-Cloud 11 Call-Off Contract (version 4)'. www.contractsfinder.service.gov.uk/Notice/Attachment/243983 (Visited 13 June 2020).
63 https://cdn-prod.opendemocracy.net/media/documents/Google_Agreement.pdf (Visited 13 June 2020).

The technology of information 107

approach.[64] The released part of the Microsoft agreement[65] is merely a general list of products and services (including the gaming platform 'Minecraft') but does not contain any specific information about the kind of involvement of the company in the project. According to the previous statement from the government, it appears that the involvement of Microsoft is limited to 'traditional' remote storage services.

It is worth mentioning, though, that on page 11 the subsection 'Limit on customer use of service output' under the provision titled 'Cognitive Services', the following appears:

> Customer will not, and will not allow third parties to use Cognitive Services or data from Cognitive Services to create, train, or improve (directly or indirectly) a similar or competing product or service.

'Cognitive Services' include recognition tools for speech, face, and handwritten recognition, as well as an 'Anomaly Detector' that 'allows you to monitor and detect abnormalities in your time series data', a 'Content Moderator' that 'provides monitoring for possible offensive, undesirable, and risky content', and 'Personalizer' that 'allows you to choose the best experience to show to your users, learning from their real-time behaviour'.[66] Once again, if these specific services are not part of the agreement with the government the language of the provision clearly points toward the critical importance of a proper training of algorithm implementations and the competitive advantage that this represents over the other players in the profiling sector.

Notwithstanding the exercise in tortuous legalese and the lack of essential information to fully understand the actual content of the services requested by the British government, it is evident that the core of the obligation is to feed algorithms with data, including personal and sensitive information. What is not entirely clear, by contrast, is whether the 'suppliers'—as the agreements call them—that provide data collection and analysis will keep a highly trained Coronavirus-related algorithm or whether they will acquire additional benefits in respect of honing the capabilities of their platforms.[67]

---

64 UK Health and Social Care Secretary's statement on coronavirus (COVID-19): 18 June 2020. www.gov.uk/government/speeches/health-and-social-care-secretarys-statement-on-coronavirus-covid-19-18-june-2020 (Visited 19 June 2020).

65 https://cdn-prod.opendemocracy.net/media/documents/Microsoft_Agreements.pdf (Visited 19 June 2020).

66 Microsoft. 'What are Azure Cognitive Services' 19 December 2020. https://docs.microsoft.com/en-us/azure/cognitive-services/welcome (Visited 19 June 2020).

67 Faculty stated that it 'asked for its contract to be amended to make clear that it will derive no commercial benefit from any software, including trained machine learning models, developed during the course of the project and that the use of the IP is under the sole control of the NHS', Shead 2020.

108 *The technology of information*

To repeat, this is a crucial point for, as we have seen in the brief account of the evolution of psychometric methods, what researchers pursue is the improvement of the efficiency of their models and algorithms by way of testing. And the possibility to train their 'AI' with real data is priceless as it gives them an edge over their competitors, but also direct control over States and governments.

Another issue to be considered is the impact of a broad automated decision-making platform in the policymaking process. This has both short-term and long-term implications. Although the phraseology of the official documents and the public statements mention the importance of keeping decisions firmly under human control[68] it is difficult to see how this can be achieved. Also even if a decision is finally deferred to a human being, the *elements* of the decision emanate from the analytics platforms, and thus from the way they work in regard to algorithm prowess, induced or hidden bias, software implementation, and so on. This means that the civil servant is required to act immediately in case of emergency and the policymaker must choose which course of action is the better one. Both need to have faith in those who designed the whole platform.

There is, needless to say, little point in advocating a ban on these technologies, especially when deployed in genuine national emergencies. As argued above, the obsession with the right to privacy has no purchase in this context. The positive evidence of their efficacy hardly provides a convincing argument in support of a principle based on dystopian fantasies. But the fact that this technology is largely in private hands is disquieting; it raises the important question of whether the State is capable of *controlling* them or able to design public policy to avoid becoming too closely tied to private interests. This, of course, is easier said than done; however, looking again at the Far East experience it may be concluded that such control is feasible, and it should be asked why in the 'civilized West' we have been unable to overcome the spread of the virus when it mattered most: at the beginning of the pandemic.

In the EU with different levels of efficiency in member states the available technology of information would have allowed the building of a similar infrastructure to be triggered in cases of emergency. It could have been achieved by feeding the various public entities with the necessary information as the British government decided to do, albeit later in its campaign. Such an infrastructure could have been assembled by allowing universities and public-funded research bodies to participate in the process from Day One. That did not occur because of the EU's cultural prejudice against the technology of information based on an irrational precautionary principle that spawned, as described in Chapter 3, a coercive and sometimes arbitrary enforcement of public order and security. The GDPR and, *a fortiori*, the draft ePrivacy regulation are perfect examples of this unhappy stance.

---

68 Bowman 2020.

The technology of information   109

Indeed, despite the official bold claims about the importance of allowing a free flow of information within the EU, data protection has become a source of *dirigiste* bureaucracy that hampers innovation and freedom of research.

Of course, the use of the technology of information to eradicate the Coronavirus implies access to an unprecedented quantity of (personal) information, and preventing its misuse is critical. Still, instead of passing a one-line provision advising member states to adopt a specific criminal offence to penalize those natural persons, legal entities, and institutions that abuse personal information, the EU chose to create a colossal and fragile construct and another 'independent authority' to prevent it from collapsing. So, when the moment of truth came, Western governments found themselves without a technology of information strategy (ignoring what information was available and what it would have been possible to achieve), a specific tactic (how specific goals could be met), and the tools of enforcement (how to the technology of information would reach the target).

Confronted with the indisputable success of Far East countries' technological approach to detection and containment, and refusing to acknowledge their superiority, Western countries exhibited the limits of their cultural framework. The immediate consequence of this lack of adaptability has been the failure of a public security model based on power rather than consent and flexibility.

References

Aratani, Lori. 2018. 'Secret Use of Census Info Helped Send Japanese Americans to Internment Camps in WWII', *Washington Post*. www.washingtonpost.com/news/retropolis/wp/2018/04/03/secret-use-of-census-info-helped-send-japanese-americans-to-internment-camps-in-wwii/ (Visited13 June 2020).

Bamford, James. 1983. *The Puzzle Palace. Inside the National Security Agency, America's Most Secret Intelligence Organization*. London: Penguin.

Banco, Erin and Spencer Ackerman. 2020. 'Team Trump Turns to Peter Thiel's Palantir to Track Virus', *Daily Beast*, 21 April. www.thedailybeast.com/trump-administration-turns-to-peter-thiels-palantir-to-track-coronavirus/body (Visited 14 June 2020).

Bernays, Edward. 1923. *Crystallizing Public Opinion*. New York: Liveright Publishing Corporation.

Bernays, Edward. 1928. *Propaganda*. New York: Liveright Publishing Corporation.

Black, Edwin. 2012. *IBM and the Holocaust: The Strategic Alliance Between Nazi Germany and America's Most Powerful Corporation*, Expanded ed. Washington: Dialog Press.

Bowman, Courtney. 2020. 'Best Practices for Using Data During a Crisis', *Palantir Blog*, 17 March. https://medium.com/palantir/best-practices-for-using-data-during-a-crisis-f2639d5eeea4 (Visited 19 June 2020).

Campbell, Duncan. 1988. 'Somebody's Listening', *New Statesman*, 12 August.

Chiccarelli, Stefano and Andrea Monti. 1997. *Spaghetti Hacker*. Milan: Felitrinelli. Second edition revised and updated, 2011, Pescara: Monti & Ambrosini.

110 *The technology of information*

Curtis, Adam. 2002a. 'The Century of Self. Episode 2 The Engineering of Consent', *BBC Two*. https://youtu.be/fEsPOt8MG7E (Visited 14 June 2020).

Curtis, Adam. 2002b. 'The Century of the Self—Part 4: Eight People Sipping Wine in Kettering', *BBC Two*, 3 May. https://youtu.be/VouaAz5mQAs (Visited 14 June 2020).

Deutsches Spionagemuseum. 'Odour Capture'. www.deutsches-spionagemuseum.d e/en/sammlung/odour-capture (Visited 13 June 2020).

Diffie, Whitfield and Martin E. Hellman. 1976. 'New Directions in Cryptography', *IEEE Transactions on Information Theory* 22(6): 644–654.

Edgar, Stacey. 2002. *Morality and Machines*, 2nd ed. Burlington: Jones & Bartlett Learning.

Fitzgerald, Mary and Cori Crider. 2020. 'Under Pressure, UK Government Releases NHS COVID Data Deals with Big Tech'. www.opendemocracy.net/en/under -pressure-uk-government-releases-nhs-covid-data-deals-big-tech/ (Visited 13 June 2020).

Fosdik, Raymond. 1915–1916. 'Passing of the Bertillon System of Identification', *Journal of the American Institute of Criminal Law and Criminology* 6(3): 363–369.

Garfinkel, Simson. 1994. *PGP. Pretty Good Privacy*. Sebastopol: O'Reilly Media.

Gould, Matthew, Indra Joshi and Ming Tang. 2020. 'The Power of Data in a Pandemic'. https://healthtech.blog.gov.uk/2020/03/28/the-power-of-data-in-a-pandemic/ (Visited 19 June 2020).

Gurven, Michael, Christopher von Rueden, Maxim Massenkoff and Hillary Kaplan. 2013. 'How Universal is the Big Five? Testing the Five-Factor Model of Personality Variation Among Forager–Farmers in the Bolivian Amazon', *Journal of Personality and Social Psychology*, 104(2): 354–370.

Hafner, Katie and John Markoff. 1995. *Cyberpunk: Outlaws and Hackers on the Computer Frontier*. New York: Touchstone.

Hinds, Joanne and Adam Joinson. 2019. 'Human and Computer Personality Prediction From Digital Footprints', *Current Directions in Psychological Science*, 28(2): 204–211. https://doi.org/10.1177/0963721419827849.

Issenberg, Sasha. 2013. *The Victory Lab. The Secret Science of Winning Campaigns*. New York: Broadway Books.

Kelion, Leo. 2013. 'Q&A: NSA's Prism Internet Surveillance Scheme', 1 July. www. bbc.com/news/technology-23051248 (Visited 13 June 2020).

Kobie, Nicholas. 2019. 'The Complicated Truth about China's Social Credit System', *Wired*, 7 June. www.wired.co.uk/article/china-social-credit-system-explained ?utm_source=More%20Stories&utm_medium=internal (Visited 17 June 2020).

Le Bon, Gustave. 1895. *Psychologie des Foules*. Paris: Alcan.

Levy, Steven. 1984. *Hackers. Heroes of the Computer Revolutions*. New York: Doubleday.

Ludlow, Peter. 1996. *High Noon on the Electronic Frontier. Conceptual Issues in Cyberspace*. Boston: A Bradford Book.

Milmo, Cahal. 2020. 'Revealed: How MI5 Recruited an Astrologer in Plot to Outwit Hitler', *The Independent*, 4 March. www.independent.co.uk/news/uk/ home-news/revealed-how-mi5-recruited-an-astrologer-in-plot-to-outwit-hitler -790876.html (Visited 13 June 2020).

Monti, Andrea and Raymond Wacks. 2019. *Protecting Personal Information: The Right to Privacy Reconsidered*. Oxford: Hart Publishing.

The technology of information   111

Mungo, Paul and Bryan Clough. 1993. *Approaching Zero: The Extraordinary Underworld of Hackers, Phreakers, Virus Writers, and Keyboard Criminals.* New York: Random House.

Nelson, Michelle. 2013. 'The Hidden Persuaders: Then and Now', *Journal of Advertising* 37: 1.

Ohmer, Susan. 2006. *George Gallup in Hollywood.* New York: Columbia University Press.

Packard, Vance. 1957. *The Hidden Persuaders.* New York: David McKay Publications.

Raymond, Eric. 1999. *The Cathedral and the Bazaar: Musings on Linux and Open Source by an Accidental Revolutionary.* Sebastopol: O'Reilly Media.

Reeves, Rosser. 1961–2017. *Reality in Advertising.* Morrisville: Lulu.com.

Rivest, Ronald, Adi Shamir and Leonard Adleman. 1978. 'A Method for Obtaining Digital Signatures and Public-Key Cryptosystems', *Communications of the ACM* 21(2). https://doi.org/10.1145/359340.359342

Sciascia, Leonardo. 1988. *Il cavaliere e la morte (Gli Adelphi).* Palermo: Adelphi.

Shah, Mohammed. 2017. '"Ford Edsel" Brand Failure Case Study and Business Lessons'. https://medium.com/@shahmm/ford-edsel-brand-failure-a-design-thin king-perspective-eea92d2e90ec (Visited 13 June 2020).

Shead, Sam. 2020. 'Britain Gave Palantir Access to Sensitive Medical Records of Covid-19 Patients in £1 DEAL', *CNBC Markets*, 8 June. www.cnbc.com/20 20/06/08/palantir-nhs-covid-19-data.html (Visited 16 June 2020).

Squire, Peverill.1988. 'Why the 1936 Literary Digest Poll Failed', *Public Opinion Quarterly* 52(1): 125–133.

Sterling, Bruce. 1992. *The Hackers' Crackdown. Law and Disorder on the Electronic Frontier.* New York: Bantam Books.

Stoll, Clifford. 1989. *The Cuckoo's Egg.* New York: Doubleday.

Wacks, Raymond. 1980. *The Protection of Privacy*, Modern Legal Studies. London: Sweet & Maxwell.

Wacks, Raymond. 1989. *Personal Information: Privacy and the Law.* Oxford: Clarendon Press.

Wacks, Raymond. 1995. *Privacy and Press Freedom.* London: Blackstone Press.

Wacks, Raymond. 2013. *Privacy and Media Freedom.* Oxford: Oxford University Press.

Williams, Sam. 2002. *Free as in Freedom: Richard Stallman's Crusade for Free Software.* O'Reilly Media: Sebastopol.

Wylie, Christopher. 2019. *Mindf*ck: Inside Cambridge Analytica's Plot to Break the World.* London: Profile Books.

Youyou, Wu, Michael Kosinski and David Stillwell. 2015. 'Computers Judge Personalities Better Than Humans', *Proceedings of the National Academy of Sciences of the United States of America* 112(4): 1036–1040. doi:10.1073/pnas.1418680112

Zimmermann, Philip. 1995. *PGP Source Code and Internals.* Boston: MIT Press.

Zuboff, Shoshana. 2019. *The Age of Surveillance Capitalism: The Fight for a Human Future at the New Frontier of Power.* New York: Public Affairs.

Zuckermann, Fredric. 1992. 'Political Police and Revolution: The Impact of the 1905 Revolution on the Tsarist Secret Police', *Journal of Contemporary History.* 2(27): 279–300.

5 The politics of the pandemic

Having no laws is a lesser evil than breaking them every day.

Ugo Foscolo[1]

The source of COVID-19 may never be known, but there is ample evidence of the political and 'scientific' failures that exacerbated its proliferation. Flawed social and economic models along with squalid living conditions clearly played a destructive part, but short-sighted political goals

> built a disease ecology whose ramifications its creators could not have begun to imagine. … nurtured urban concentrations whose density had never been seen before and would not be seen for centuries thereafter … facilitated movement and connectivity within its unusually wide and diverse geographical regions. The scale of environmental transformation … represented the greatest surge of ecological change between the Neolithic and Industrial Revolutions. The commercial networks binding … to peoples beyond the frontier, especially in Africa and Asia, appear stronger than we had ever imagined. And outside of human control, after a period of stability … a phase of raucous climate disorganization began.[2]

Nor was the drive to overcome the virus assisted by the pontifications of self-important scientists, wild rumours, fake news, and the dramatic impact on the economy.

This description may sound like an account of COVID-19; it is actually an account of the smallpox epidemic of 165 during the Roman Empire (mentioned in Chapter 1) which extended as far as China.[3] The virus spread to Rome by the legions returning from the Middle East campaign against the Parthians, and which almost wiped them out. The epidemic also

---

1 Foscolo, Ugo. 1860. Translated by Andrea Monti.
2 Harper 2019: 72.
3 Duncan-Jones 2018: 44–45.

The politics of the pandemic   113

devastated the population that either resorted to magic and superstition—like those endorsed by the bogus physician and *ante litteram*, Alexander of Abonoteichus—to exorcize the 'evil' or turned to monotheistic cults (mainly Christianity) in an attempt to comprehend the pain they were suffering. Even the great Galen, the 'egotistical, arrogant, bossy, bombastic ... unapologetic owner of slaves and possibly ... misogynist[4] escaped from Rome at the very start of the contagion, powerless against the virus'. He returned a few years later, summoned by the Emperor Marcus Aurelius, but did little more than describe the disease and face its dire consequences:

> Galen thought there were remedies to blunt the force of the disease, but these are a register of pure desperation: milk from mountain cattle, Armenian dirt, the urine of a boy. The mortality event he lived through stands as not only perhaps the first pandemic in human history, but also a moment of rupture in the story of the Roman Empire.[5]

The risk of internal disorders led the Emperor to increase the worshipping of the traditional religion to keep citizens at bay. This was achieved by pragmatically promoting the traditional religion and condemning the 'foreign cults' that challenged the authority of the supreme ruler. 'Science' and superstition played an essential role during the pandemic: Emperor Marcus Aurelius asked Galen for help, but also resorted to the chicanery of the fraudulent Alexander of Abonoteichus, founder of the sham Glycon cult which consisted of the worship of a snake-human-headed god allegedly a reincarnation of Aesculapius.

Alexander's 'spell'—*Phoebus, the god unshorn, keepeth off plague's nebulous onset*—was carved on the wooden doors as a talisman against the plague. Its supposed 'power' did not, of course, halt the plague. In fact it spread more rapidly precisely because of people's negligence in seeking to avoid infection, supported by the false creed of being 'immune'. The charlatan's influence did not even end at citizens' doors: during the plague the legions were fighting the Danube battle against the Marcomanni tribes and the Emperor asked Alexander for an oracle to divine the victory. He called for the sacrifice of two lions to be drowned in the river. But his spell was evidently ineffective and notwithstanding the rite, the battle was a major disaster, and he escaped the consequences of his false oracle thanks to his wheedling and pedantry.

Although he was the most successful, Alexander of Abonoteichus was not the only one who exploited the ignorance and fear of the population:

4 Mattern 2018: 284.
5 Harper: 24.

114 *The politics of the pandemic*

[E]very day more charlatans and madmen appeared in Rome, preying on the gullible. One of the most notorious ones had been constantly preaching to the crowds from atop the wild fig-tree on the Campus Martius. He was on the verge of starting looting in the streets of Rome by prophesying that any day the gods were about to send down fire from the heavens to engulf the city and that the end of the world was nigh. He predicted that he would be transformed into a stork when the apocalypse was upon them and tried to dupe the crowds by falling from the tree and releasing a bird concealed beneath his cloak. They saw through this hopeless ruse, though, and he was brought before the emperor for judgement. Marcus quickly surmised that he was touched by madness, and pardoned him without a fuss. The last thing he wanted was to make martyrs out of these religious lunatics.[6]

The economy suffered so badly that the government was compelled to increase taxes that people were, in any event, unable to pay. As a result they escaped from villages to 'hide' in the cities so the production of wheat, oil, and wine fell significantly. In Rome the daily death toll was so high that it became impossible to bury the dead.

On the Eastern border, with the legions having been almost destroyed by the plague, the Emperor enlisted gladiators and slaves—the *Volountarii*—with the promise of compensating them for their service with their freedom. He was also forced to accept as landlords the defeated Marcomanni tribes using them as 'buffers' between the borders of the Empire and the outlying territories. This marked the beginning of the dissolution of the Roman Empire that was no longer able to rule with autonomous power.[7] The general consensus is that the pandemic unleashed a deadly chain reaction throughout the whole Empire and at all levels of society.[8]

A closer look at the challenges faced by Emperor Marcus Aurelius and his (by all accounts, less capable) successors confronting the effects of the plague displays striking parallels with COVID-19. At the beginning of the pandemic the chief priority was preserving the survival of the Empire. Marcus Aurelius kept his focus on maintaining the social structure and institutions. The loss of life that was affecting the administrative efficiency of the Empire was confronted by allowing foreigners and *cives* belonging to a lower stratum to become an active part of the ruling offices. In the short term, his objects included the recovery of the efficacy of the military apparatus, retarding economic collapse, and, possibly the greatest challenge, attempting to manage 'public order' with all the available social tools. And when nothing more could be done, he accepted the existence of the plague

---

6 Robertson 2020.
7 Sabbatani & Fiorino 2009: 261–275.
8 For a contrary view, see Bruun 2012: 123–165.

The politics of the pandemic   115

as a fact of life. 'Remember', he wrote, 'every duty is the sum of certain parts. To perform it in an orderly manner, it is necessary to observe them, and without fussing at all, nor responding to anger with anger'.[9]

His son and direct successor Commodus, as well as other emperors, did not prove as capable in managing the consequences of the Antonine Plague and of the subsequent Cyprian Plague (AD 249). They preserved the exteriority of the Empire but progressively lost its substance, while people continued looking with growing interest at the salvific promise of the rising Christian monotheism.

Science and superstition

While any plague cannot be the exclusive cause of the disruption of the then world order, it is unquestionable that (the lack of) scientific knowledge and superstition played an essential role in shaping Imperial public policies in the same way they have done in the case of COVID-19. As in the case of the Imperial plagues, the more a State exhibits a limited capability to cope with the social consequences of a pandemic, the higher the risk of a breach of the social contract and the return of the *homo, homini lupus* condition. The ubiquitous panic-buying and the riots caused by or in the name of the pandemic are reliable witnesses of this phenomenon.

From another perspective, as in the past, the desperate need to 'know', 'understand', and 'foresee' has a pivotal role in the management of public policy. It is not therefore surprising to meet the heirs of Galen and Alexander of Abonoteichus at the court of the new emperors that, like their predecessors, have been lured into the 'magic power' of predictive technology and 'artificial intelligence', while the public all too easily fall prey to a latter-day Glyconian cult. In the United States, for example, between March and July 2020 the Food and Drug Administration issued 79 warning letters against companies selling a wide range of 'cures' including Coronavirus boneset tea, colloidal silver, cannabidiol and salt therapy products, homeopathic and Ayurvedic drugs:[10]

> There Are No Vaccines or Medicines for COVID-19, Yet these fraudulent products that claim to cure, treat, or prevent COVID-19 haven't been evaluated by the FDA for safety and effectiveness and might be dangerous to you and your family.
>
> The FDA is particularly concerned that these deceptive and misleading products might cause Americans to delay or stop appropriate

---

9   Marcus Aurelius, Τὰ εἰς ἑαυτόν VI, 26. Translated from the Italian by Andrea Monti.
10 US Food and Drug Administration. 2020. 'Fraudulent Coronavirus Disease 2019 (COVID-19) Products'. www.fda.gov/consumers/health-fraud-scams/fraudulent-coronavirus-disease-2019-covid-19-products#Warning%20Letter%20Table (Visited 4 July 2020).

116 *The politics of the pandemic*

medical treatment, leading to serious and life-threatening harm. It's likely that the products do not do what they claim, and the ingredients in them could cause adverse effects and could interact with, and potentially interfere with, essential medications.[11]

This caution was not, however, evinced by other sectors of the US government; indeed, President Donald Trump was accused by the scientific press of having

... given the nation and desperate patients false hope about what options are widely available to treat those fighting for their lives. By suggesting that these drugs are sitting on shelves just waiting to be used, the president will increase public demand for medicines that may not be safe, effective, in abundant supply or wise to use right now.[12]

This is not merely a Western peculiarity; in India, a politician promoted a cure identical to that suggested by Galen some two thousand years ago:

[A] party worker from the ruling Bharatiya Janata Party in the state of West Bengal organized a cow urine consumption event to protect people from infection. Other public voices have endorsed the view that cow urine functions as an elixir, effective not only in warding off COVID-19 but diseases such as cancer, diabetes and heart attacks.[13]

Have we really progressed from the times of Alexander the Charlatan? The answer is of the utmost importance, as public policy is increasingly dependent upon data and science, and the Coronavirus pandemic has demonstrated that the lack of scientific knowledge imparted by our systems of education affects the soundness of a choice and the effectiveness its implementation.

The media

Yet again we cannot overstate the role of traditional media and digital platforms (be they a search engine, a social networking provider, or a software manufacturer) in shaping public opinion. In fact, in the West, the media offers numerous scientific programmes or science-based content. On the other hand, in less science-oriented societies, the media devote significantly

---

11 US Food and Drug Administration. 2020. 'Beware of Fraudulent Coronavirus Tests, Vaccines and Treatments'. www.fda.gov/consumers/consumer-updates/beware-fraudulent-cor onavirus-tests-vaccines-and-treatments (Visited 4 July 2020).

12 McBride-Folkers & Caplan 2020.

13 Mir, Raoof, 'India's media must promote science, not superstition, in COVID-19 fight'. *Nikkei Asian Review* 6 April 2020. https://asia.nikkei.com/Opinion/India-s-media-must -promote-science-not-Csuperstition-in-COVID-19-fight (Visited 4 July 2020).

The politics of the pandemic   117

less time to fostering a scientific culture, while social media are largely dominated by entertainment:

> [P]owerful new electronic media have on the contrary largely failed to perform this role to its full potential ... Much of the media in India is controlled by large, for-profit corporations in the absence of restrictions on cross-media ownership. These companies therefore prioritize economic growth and business interests over the other democratic functions of media, encouraging consumerism, entertainment and self-gratification. For the few who want information about scientific knowledge in India, they have to seek it out and pay for it, whereas news about cricket, politics and entertainment easily finds its way to audiences through social media and television. The fascination with entertainment-driven content shapes people's mindsets and makes them more likely to believe what these programs say, which tends to be unscientific or even hostile to science.[14]

The fanciful conspiracy theories about 5G technology as a cause of Coronavirus and the existence of a global plot to prevent access of a vaccine to all citizens spread so effectively in Europe that the EU institutions had to issue a public statement to expose the falsity:

> There is no connection between 5G and the coronavirus. The coronavirus is spread from one person to another through droplets that people sneeze, cough or exhale. 5G is the new generation of mobile network technology that is transmitted over non-ionising radio waves. There is no evidence that 5G is harmful to people's health. The outbreak of coronavirus in the Chinese city of Wuhan is unrelated to 5G, and is thought to have originated in a seafood wholesale market ... No, Bill Gates is not the creator of the coronavirus, and he is not plotting with the EU to create a global surveillance system to track the movements of people. This is a well-known conspiracy theory and there is no evidence to back it up.[15]

This did not, however, achieve the desired effect. Specious and unfounded theories still flourish, and the media seem content to broadcast them. The need to control or regulate the propagation of fake news is a pressing matter that lies beyond the scope of these pages. It is worth repeating, however, that—as discussed in Chapter 4—today's world of thought control is far more complicated than in the days of the State-controlled propaganda.

---

14 Ibid.
15 EU Commission. 'Separating fact from fiction'. https://ec.europa.eu/info/live-work-trav el-eu/health/coronavirus-response/fighting-disinformation_en (Visited 4 July 2020).

118 *The politics of the pandemic*

Western countries have generally eschewed the 'old school' forms of censorship; it has been replaced by the social-networking-enhanced balkanization of public opinion, where for every statement there is its opposite, equally valid, and no less convincing to the followers of the ever-expanding group of online 'influencers'. As a result, notwithstanding the publicly proclaimed public sector's good intentions, the deluge of misinformation governs every available space in the public square and in the minds of individuals. Misinformation that emanates from a 'friendly' source is usually presented in an easily digested, plausible form that appears to be based on reputable and verifiable 'findings':

> The internet provides us with seemingly limitless data ... that could in theory enhance our intelligence and enable us to become more knowledgeable, to be more skilful or to otherwise use actionable intelligence. Maybe we could improve our decision-making, reflect on our beliefs, interrogate our own biases, and so on. But do we? Who does? Who exactly is made smarter? And how? And with respect to what? Are you and I ... more intelligent? Or ... Do we find ourselves mindlessly following scripts written or designed by others? We're easily led to believe that we're extending our minds and becoming more intelligent with a little help from the digital tech tools, when in reality, those are often just illusions, sales pitches optimized to pave the path of least resistance.[16]

The problem seems intractable. It is not enough to recognize that digital robber barons collect personal information to shape the way we think and act.[17] As suggested in the previous chapter, education is the strongest defence against any consent-manufacture and psychologically based manipulation. It provides individuals the ability to distinguish between their genuine and fabricated choices or views. The media also have an essential role in delivering reliable information rather than engaging in morbid speculation about the pandemic. The relationship between science and the media is complex. The media are desperately hungry to reveal the latest scientific breakthrough, and researchers need publicity to satisfy their egos, build their reputation, and, most importantly, to attract funds for their research projects. This convergence of interests often leads to the media to present preliminary or early-stage research as if it were already accomplished.

This is not simply a matter of taste or propriety. There is a serious negative impact on policymakers from 'scientific' fake news, the publication of withdrawn scientific papers, exaggerated appraisals of the pandemic, the fatality rates, misuse of the 'exponential' concept, the adoption of non-evidence

16 Frischmann 2020.
17 Monti & Wacks 2019: 52.

The politics of the pandemic   119

based extreme measures, resource misallocation, and several other factors in the transition from science to public policy through the media:[18]

> Based on Altmetric scores, the most discussed and most visible scientific paper across all 20+ million papers published in the last 8 years across all science is a preprint claiming that the new coronavirus' spike protein bears 'uncanny similarity' with HIV-1 proteins.
>
> The Altmetric score of this work has reached an astronomical level of 13 725 points as of 5 March 2020. The paper was rapidly criticized as highly flawed, and the authors withdrew it within days. Regardless, major harm was already done. The preprint fuelled conspiracy theories of scientists manufacturing dangerous viruses and offered ammunition to vaccine deniers. Refutation will probably not stop dispersion of weird inferences. The first report documenting transmission by an asymptomatic individual was published in the *New England Journal of Medicine* on January 30. However, the specific patient did have symptoms, but researchers had not asked. Understanding the chances of transmission during the asymptomatic phase has major implications for what protective measures might work. *The Lancet* published on February 24 an account from two Chinese nurses of their front-line experience fighting coronavirus. The authors soon retracted the paper admitting it was not a first-hand account.[19] (Ioannidis, 2020, p. 1)

The media and 'professional plotters' have not been the only (self-conscious, concurring) victims of this unreliable 'scientific' news: many Western policymakers have fallen prey to the precautionary-principle paranoia:

> Many countries pass legislation that allocates major resources and funding to the coronavirus response. This is justified, but the exact allocation priorities can become irrational. For example, undoubtedly research on coronavirus vaccines and potential treatments must be accelerated. However, if only part of resources mobilized to implement extreme measures for COVID-19 had been invested towards enhancing influenza vaccination uptake, tens of thousands of influenza deaths might have been averted ... enhanced detection of infections and lower hospitalization thresholds may increase demands for hospital beds. For patients without severe symptoms, hospitalizations offer no benefit and may only infect health workers causing shortage of much-needed personnel ... Excess admissions may strain health care systems and increase

18 Ioannidis 2020.
19 Op. cit., 1.

120 *The politics of the pandemic*

mortality from other serious diseases where hospital care is clearly effective.[20]

One is reminded of Don Ferrante, the 'martyr of the useless doctrine and formal logic',[21] a minor fictional character in Alessandro Manzoni's *I Promessi Sposi*. In 1630 the plague was devastating the Duchy of Milan and while the peasants were succumbing to the disease, Don Ferrante believed that his mastery of Aristotelian logic would protect him against infection:

> In rerum natura ... there are but two kinds of things: substances and accidents; and if I prove that the contagion can neither be one nor the other of these, I shall have proved that it does not exist; that it is a chimera.[22]

He was badly mistaken. He died from the virus.

On the other hand, those who applied critical thinking saw clearly through the fog of the political instrumentalism of the pandemic, from the United States vs China Cold War II, to the *revanche* of separatist movements in various continents, and the attempt of local authorities to usurp the powers of central governments. As a result in those Western countries where the government ruled by authority rather than *gravitas*, the people did not 'feel' bound to comply with regulation. They decided instead to accept the validity of the latest 'logical' and 'indisputable' confirmation of a 'global plot' or were paralyzed by an overwhelming nihilism. And all the while economies crashed, ruining the lives of millions.

Democratic societies depend on compliance with regulation. In the absence of co-operation, a degree of pressure is inevitable. When this fails greater coercion is required to protect lives. This step may risk undermining the legitimacy of the State and the rule of law, and raises fundamental questions about the integrity of the law and legal system in times of genuine emergency.

The rule of law

The rule of law is an indispensable means by which rights are secured—especially during a crisis of the sort generated by the Coronavirus. It is therefore crucial that it be defended when emergencies arise. But is it enough? The enforcement of unpopular and occasionally Draconian regulations may generate the destabilization of society. The imposition of fines or even imprisonment may be inadequate to ensure compliance with the

---

20 Op. cit., 2.
21 Donadoni 1963: Translation by Andrea Monti.
22 Manzoni 1827: 441–442.

law. Pandemic-related public policy is targeted toward the entire population and not merely deviant or criminal individuals. Without widespread spontaneous acquiescence, the government has little choice but to consider coercing all in order to contain the malfeasance of the few. This may require a reconsideration of our conception of the rule of law and the protection of individual rights under circumstances of extreme emergency.

If a certain regulation prevents immediate action to save lives, what is wrong is the specific legislation and not the *principle* of the rule of law:

> Where governments respond with an expanded role and the forceful presence of police and other security actors, challenges can emerge, including perceptions of bias, disproportionate use of force, and other human rights issues. There is also a risk that some states may utilize emergency powers to consolidate executive authority at the expense of the rule of law, suppressing dissent and undermining democratic institutions, especially where courts and other oversight bodies struggle to perform due to COVID-related restrictions.[23]

The Diceyan concept of the rule of law is a formal, procedural notion that rests on three institutional and constitutional requirements without specifying what the content of the law ought to be.[24] The first principle declares that no one is punishable except for a distinct breach of law established in the ordinary legal manner before the ordinary courts of the land. The rule of law is thereby differentiated from systems of government based on the exercise of wide, arbitrary, or discretionary powers. Dicey's reference to wide, arbitrary, or discretionary powers could extend to laws that infringe fundamental rights, or it could describe laws properly enacted, but which are vague or uncertain so that citizens are unable to plan their lives in accord with the law.

The second principle states that everyone regardless of rank or status is subject to the ordinary law and amenable to the jurisdiction of the ordinary courts. This is a formal or institutional notion rather than a substantive concern with how judges actually apply the law to different individuals or groups. The third principle is that the values of the constitution (for example the right to personal liberty, or the right of public hearing) are the result of judicial decisions determining the rights of private persons in particular cases before the courts.

Jurists have attempted to adapt the Diceyan conception of the rule of law to contemporary questions of legality, authority, and other virtues of

---

23 Zouev 2020.
24 Dicey 1885.

122 *The politics of the pandemic*

democratic governance.[25] While a formal (or content-neutral) conception of the rule of law allows us to appraise a legal system independently of its political or moral quality, from the point of view of justice, a wicked legal system could satisfy these formal norms while enacting unjust laws. Many commentators and politicians, however, conceive the rule of law as the means by which to preserve the democratic values of society. A way out of this dilemma may be to accept, as Joseph Raz has recently suggested, that the rule of law's purpose is to prevent arbitrary government. He contends that it requires that government action demonstrates the intention to defend and advance the interests of the governed. It therefore becomes a near essential condition for the law to satisfy *other moral demands*, and it operates as a coordinating and cooperative force both domestically and internationally.

This approach is to be found in several legal systems such as France, Italy, and England that—albeit with a few nuances—defer to the concept of public order the role of embodying those 'national interests that are essential to maintain an ordered civil coexistence'.[26] In this case, though, ethical issues may be irrelevant because the idea of 'core values' is sufficiently flexible either to sustain the legality of affirming or denying, say, capital punishment as a vital component of a 'democratic' society. This approach allows a degree of normativity by which fundamental rights can attain legal status if they are acknowledged as one the 'core values' of a State. They thus become a structural component of the rule of law in the sense that fundamental rights exert a restriction on the naked power of the ruler. It does not, however, sidestep the question of who decides what these 'core values' are.

The courts

One of the surest methods of eviscerating the rule of law is to oust the jurisdiction of judges over executive action. Quoting Socrates, Ernst Fraenkel commences his seminal work, *The Dual State*, with this question:

---

25 For example, Lon Fuller's idea of the 'inner morality of law' specifies eight desiderata with which the law should comply if it is to achieve 'excellence'. See Fuller 1969. Joseph Raz attempts to add flesh to the bones of Dicey's principles, but emphasizes that the rule of law is not the sole virtue of a legal system. See Raz 1977. His organizing principle is that the rule of law performs a crucial role in facilitating individuals planning their lives. To do so the law ought to be prospective (as opposed to retrospective) and relatively stable; that particular laws should be directed by open, general, and clear rules; that the courts should be independent and accessible; and that those who enforce the law should not have untrammelled discretion. See too Raz 2019; Grant 2017; Dworkin 1986; Craig 1997; Bingham 2010.

26 *Corte costituzionale*, 2001. Decision 25 July 2001, n. 290. www.giurcost.org/decision i/2001/0290s-01.html (Visited 10 July 2020).

The politics of the pandemic   123

Do you believe that a state in which the decisions of the courts can have no validity, but can be reversed and nullified by particular persons, would subsist rather than perish?[27]

Fraenkel's anxiety related to Hitler's relentless efforts to sever judicial control over the Nazi party and to affirm the total autonomy (and power) of the former over the legal system as a whole. In this two-stage *coup*, the first goal was to abolish the rule of law:

> The National-Socialist *coup d'état* consisted in the fact that the National-Socialists, as the dominant party in the government, (1) did not prevent but rather caused the infringement of the Rule of Law, (2) abused the state of martial law which they had fraudulently promoted in order to abolish the Constitution, and (3) now maintain a state of martial law despite their assurances that Germany, in the midst of a world corrupt with inner strife, is an 'island of peace'.[28]

By succeeding in this goal, the Gestapo was given free rein to enforce the rule of the Party (or, in effect, the Fuhrer) without the fetters of the rule of law, the separation of powers, and other institutions that stood in the way of the exercise of unrestrained power.[29] To achieve the wholesale dismantling of the rule of law it was necessary to ensure that courts could not intervene to limit, even on a limited basis, the policing power of the party. This was achieved by abolishing judicial review of Gestapo actions as a consequence of the declared 'martial law'. As Fraenkel points out, citing an English authority:[30]

> Martial law, when applied to the civilian, is no law at all, but a shadowy, uncertain, precarious something depending entirely on the conscience, or rather, on the despotic and arbitrary rule of those who administer it.[31]

To summarize, the rule of law may be crushed by three attacks: the imposition of martial law as a consequence of a state of emergency, the ouster of judicial review of the declaration of martial law, and the transformation of this 'exception' into a 'new legal normality'. In this strategy, socially shared values are the catalyst that creates a chain reaction which smooths the way toward the demise of democracy. Thus those who control values, ultimately

---

27 Fraenkel 1941: 2.
28 Ibid, 10.
29 See the references in note 70, Chapter 3 Chapter for a discussion of South African apartheid legislation that successfully ousted the courts' jurisdiction over, for example, detention.
30 Cockburn 1867: 86.
31 Ibid, 24.

124 *The politics of the pandemic*

control power, regardless of the rule of law. Hence the vital importance of social control tools: propaganda and shepherding techniques, such as nudging, to lure, rather than oblige, citizens into compliance.

But this conclusion is valid if—and only if—certain values are shared by the whole community. Such a moral consensus may require the control, or even the eradication, of beliefs that run counter to this consensus. This control is achieved mainly by limiting free speech: if ideas cannot be expressed they cannot spread, and if they are properly contained the 'core values' of the State remain intact. Cracking down on dissenting opinion implies, as a corollary, the infringement of the right to privacy and other fundamental rights. The more the State's 'core values' coincide with socially accepted creeds, the less relevant are laws and regulations because the will of the people is the will of the governing party and vice versa. By contrast, the more distant the social values are from State's values, the more the rule of law loses its significance.

In this regard, freedom of expression is obviously of fundamental importance in preserving and defending democratic values. Information technology continues to play a central role in disturbing the balance between freedom and anarchy. It is now a given that social networking platforms (be they web-based profile pages or a smartphone-powered messaging group) have caused the balkanization of public opinion by allowing a myriad cult-like groups—or even single individuals—to imagine they have an important contribution to make to public policy. The effect has generally been to unsettle the behaviour of institutions, companies, and, ultimately, of citizens themselves.[32]

We are facing an unprecedented clash between (tribal) values and the law, between (personal) ethics and rights, with many Western societies unwilling to shake off the chains of political correctness, incapable of acting in their capacity as cultural mediators. Statues are demolished, images recast, language 'reformed', books and films proscribed. The inventory of the unacceptable grows by the day. If social values are so powerful as to produce direct and immediate modification of the behaviour of public institutions and corporations without the need for reform of public policy, it may be not be perverse to enquire whether it might be preferable to live in a society governed by values than one based on the rule of law!

China is a contemporary example of the former: laws are important, but not to the extent of being a restraint on the will of the Communist Party. In contrast to the approach of the Third Reich where the prerogative State was *legibus solutus* (not handcuffed by the law) and *superiorem non*

---

32 See the open letter to *Harper's Magazine* signed by some 150 prominent writers, artists, academics, and journalists, 'A Letter on Justice and Open Debate', *Harper's Magazine* 7 July 2020. https://harpers.org/a-letter-on-justice-and-open-debate/ (Visited 13 July 2020).

The politics of the pandemic 125

recognoscens (acknowledging no superior authority), China has enforced a 'rule by law' rather than by a 'rule of law' doctrine:

> The original *fǎ zhì* (法制) principle was reformulated into *fǎ zhì* (法治); the difference in the two homophone *zhi* characters may only be seen when reading the Chinese characters, and is quite relevant: the first *zhì* (制) means 'system', whereas the second one (治) is associated to the idea of harnessing, managing or governing—*fǎ zhì* (法治) thus implying a notion of an instrumental relation between the two terms: one which may either be translated as 'rule of law' or as 'rule by law'.[33]

The difference between 'rule of law' and 'rule by law' may be subtle, but is still substantial. If law is but a tool to rule and not a limit to the power of the State, whatever 'pleases' the ruling élite becomes mandatory and enforced nonetheless. In China this process is well active and evolving.

> Subsequent developments eventually proved that the more 'liberal' attitudes displayed towards 'the rule of law' by the ruling élite in the 1990s receded in importance, with a softening of legality principles promoted by the leadership in the following decade, with a view to the construction of a 'socialist harmonious society'.[34]

The word 'harmonious' suggests a peculiarity of Chinese socialist rule, its deep-rooted Confucian origin, and the prevalence of a moral hierarchy over the 'mere' law abiding. In short, the evolution of Confucian doctrine led to the affirmation of Mencius' theory according to which 'it is the explicit responsibility of the ruler ... to assist his subjects in their efforts to keep to the right path. To this end, the ruler is enjoined ... to provide for the material well-being of his people'.[35] The impact of the market economy and the need to enforce strong social control and the inevitable injection (or infection, from the party's perspective) of Western values (along with the problems posed by the absorption of Hong Kong into the motherland) produced threats to the 'traditional' Confucian/communist rule whose resolution remains a long way off. Nevertheless, the results achieved by China in apparently containing the pandemic led many observers to ask whether 'Asian values' (the Confucian-based beliefs that afford a shared basis for Asian countries) have proved superior to the rule of law, fundamental rights-centred, individualist Western legal systems.

It seems clear that neo-Confucianism in its authoritarian form played a role China's management of the crisis. But it is at least questionable whether

33 Castellucci 2012: 14.
34 Op. cit., 15.
35 Gardner 2014: 54.

126 *The politics of the pandemic*

'Asian values' actually exist.[36] Moreover, it is doubtful whether the successes achieved by other Far East nations are directly attributable to the adoption or application of these putative principles. First, 'Asia' is an anthropological notion that is more complex than China, Japan, and—more recently, from a Western perspective—South Korea. Second, although in the past Chinese cultural influence has been robust, it does not follow that it is still strong, or even exists, beyond mainland China. Third, linking 'Asian values' to Confucianism, and excluding India and Buddhism, neglects the enormous complexity of Asian anthropology.

Japan's 'mysteriously low virus death rate'[37] appears to have been the result of an effective, slow-paced strategy that avoided the sorts of hostile debates witnessed in Europe and the United States regarding the risk to fundamental rights or lowering the standard of democracy. Together with a high level of spontaneous compliance with the 'stay-at-home' recommendation issued by the government (that chose not to adopt legal regulation) the culturally ingrained distancing and mask-wearing tradition and the contact tracing system in place since 1950 to eradicate tuberculosis aided efforts to break the chain of the contagion. Despite the state of emergency declared on 7 April 2020, no Draconian regulations affecting either the rule of law or fundamental rights were enacted, and the need to process personal data from the national health system and from private corporations was successfully harmonized with the protection of personal information:

> On 27 March 2020, Ministry of Health, Labour and Welfare with other Ministries called for a collaboration with the social media companies to conduct survey of health conditions. LINE, a social media company, with 83 million users which amounts nearly 67 percent of the Japanese population, contributed to this survey in April 2020. Approximately 30 percent of the users responded this survey. This survey focuses on the fever of each user to predict the spread of Covid-19. The other major mobile phone companies also assisted the big data analytics from the spatial statics data to appear the people's movement. These companies have taken care of the users' privacy.[38]

And South Korea's experience was equally positive:

> [S]ome media have offered reductive cultural explanations for this success. A common trope is that Koreans are less individualistic, more community-oriented, and more willing to sacrifice for the greater good

---

36 Kim 2010.
37 Wingfield-Hayes 2020.
38 Miyashita, Hiroshi 2020. Covid-19 and Data Protection in Japan 27 July 2020. https://blogdroiteuropeen.com/ (Visited 27 July 2020).

The politics of the pandemic 127

... This is nonsense, and it repeats the same mistake that allowed the rampant coronavirus outbreaks in the United States and Europe in the first place: the mistake of seeing Asia as an unrelatable other, a place so fundamentally different from the West that no knowledge or experience is transferable.[39]

In fact, as pointed out by Park, South Korea ranks below several Western countries in the mutual trust chart;[40] in the political arena, lawmakers occasionally resort to fisticuffs, fake news and spying to influence elections, and, during the pandemic, the pressure of a stakeholder association, whose president has ties with right wing movements, managed to stop a leading expert advising the government:

> Koreans are as schooled in their own liberty as anyone else. And, as with most people, they have been willing to accept small intrusions to reduce the likelihood of infection. ... Far from being obedient, the Koreans are, on the contrary, so fractious and disobedient that it takes some effort to get them to acquiesce ... In free South Korea, this fractiousness has resulted in a view of democracy that posits that it is the job of politicians to make real the will of the people, rather than act as delegates representing a majority of their constituency ... A real screwup with COVID-19 could have resulted in a serious move to impeach. Such a prospect naturally focuses presidential thinking on results.[41]

Culture plainly played a significant role in the citizens' response to the measures adopted by the government. But the heart of the matter is the efficacy of leadership:

> South Korea's success is thanks to competent leadership that inspired public trust. No sacred Confucian text advised Korean health officials to summon medical companies and told them to ramp up testing capacity when Korea had only four known cases of COVID-19. No Asian wisdom made Korean doctors think they should test everyone with pneumonia symptoms regardless of travel history, which led to the discovery of the now infamous 'Patient 31' and the suppression of the massive coronavirus cluster in the city of Daegu caused by the secretive Shincheonji cult. The South Korean public isn't hoarding toilet paper not because they are sheep with no individual agency but because they

---

39 Park 2020.
40 Stiglitz, Fitoussi, & Durand 2018.
41 Breen 2020.

128 *The politics of the pandemic*

plainly saw that their government was committed to being transparent and trusted it to act in their interest.[42]

In a nutshell, South Korea responded swiftly to the pandemic because, 'It's about civic memory, not Confucius ... We remember MERS. We remember other epidemics. We know this is a marathon. But we're in a better place because the entire society has been in this game, fighting together'.[43]

Other 'Third World' nations such as Senegal and the Indian state of Kerala have been 'surprisingly' effective in containing the virus, while the experience of two of the world's superpowers was abysmal:

> They ignored the threat. When they were forced to act, they sent mixed signals to citizens which encouraged many to act in ways which spread the infection. Neither did anything like the testing needed to control the virus. Both failed to equip their hospitals and health workers with the equipment they needed, triggering many avoidable deaths.
>
> The failure was political. The US is the only rich country with no national health system ... Britain's much-loved National Health Service has been weakened by spending cuts. Both governments failed to fight the virus in time because they had other priorities.[44]

Italy

The Italian example is instructive. Along with South Korea, but from the opposite position, it represents a 'bookend'.[45] Leaving aside other structural problems that afflict the country, the authorities underestimated the gravity of the threat, and their response was indecisive and tardy. Communication with the public was muddled and, most importantly, there was inadequate preparation, despite the existence of a pandemic emergency plan[46] which ought to have been ready to be launched immediately. These factors combined to produce a huge death toll, but crippled the economy and debilitated the constitutional order.

The Byzantine complexity of the government's efforts involved a convoluted panoply of laws, decrees of the president of the council, decrees, governmental FAQs and guidelines, regional presidents' and mayors' ordinances.[47]

---

42 Park 2020.
43 Thompson 2020.
44 Friedman 2020.
45 Martin & Walker 2020.
46 Ministero della Salute. 2018. Piano nazionale di preparazione e risposta ad una pandemia influenzale. www.salute.gov.it/imgs/C_17_pubblicazioni_501_allegato.pdf (Visited 13 July 2020).
47 Italian Camera dei Deputati. 'Misure sull'emergenza coronavirus (COVID-19)—Quadro generale' 27 June 2020. https://temi.camera.it/leg18/temi/iniziative-per-prevenire-e-cont

The politics of the pandemic   129

Eminent scholars have supported the approach adopted by the government toward the legal framework constructed by parliament and government.[48] The State was not subjected to anything approaching a *coup*, and Italy has retained its democratic character because no actual turn from the normative state to the prerogative state has been attempted. Nonetheless, there remain several unresolved matters such as the *de facto* (permanent) extension of the powers of the president of the council to limit constitutional rights, the balkanization of the regional powers against the central government, and the still unclear relationship between public security and health emergencies.[49]

What is especially intriguing about the Italian experience is the approach to fundamental rights, particularly the right to privacy. Being, like many countries, in a state of denial, the Italian government delayed the response to the disease until 26 February 2020 by which time only rigorous measures could serve the purpose of controlling its spread. In an attempt to buttress this decision the lockdown was introduced gradually rather than in a single declaration. This squandered valuable time available to act decisively. The social fatigue imposed by compliance to the lockdown order and the lack of attention to questions of public order (panic buying, quarantine, and social distancing infringements, the near obliteration of judicial activity), and the failure properly to use the available technology generated a futile implementation of heavy-handed security.

It was not merely the hysteria in Western countries that impeded the use of information technology in the management of the pandemic. Nor in Italy was it only the traditional attitude toward any form of regulation— *fatta la legge, trovato l'inganno* (every law has its loophole). The key failure was the absence of a long-term strategy of technology policing. As argued in Chapter 3, the fundamental question is that either digital exposure notification or a full contact tracing or a geo-fencing-based quarantine computer programme requires the cooperation (or better still, the authorization) of the two US Big Tech corporations that control the smartphone operating systems. Moreover, notwithstanding the wide availability of free and open source software that provide technical, economic, and political independence in the use of computer operating systems, databases, and Internet-related platforms, the pandemic engendered an increase in the use of proprietary software within the civil service and the judiciary—where remote court hearings are only possible by way of *Skype for Business* and *Teams*[50]—universities and schools:

rastare-la-diffusione-del-nuovo-coronavirus.html (Visited 14 July 2020).

48 Luciani 2020.

49 Monti 2020.

50 Ministero della giustizia, Dipartimento dell'organizzazione giudiziaria del personale e dei servizi, Direzione generale per i sistemi informativi automatizzati. 20 marzo 2020. http://pst.giustizia.it/PST/resources/cms/documents/provvedimento_organizzativo_dgsia_ex.pdf (Visited 17 July 2020).

130 *The politics of the pandemic*

> From the first of July the institutional email accounts of the Italian school pass to Microsoft. This was decided by the Ministry of Education, which in recent days has sent a circular between the institutions to announce the migration of the accounts of schools and executives on Office 365, the cloud platform of the American company that collects e-mail services, shared work and video calls.[51]

Not everything was actually handed out *gratis*, but Big Tech took advantage of the usual 'free-as-in-free-beer' strategy by permitting countries to use their products and services free of charge or at a reduced cost 'because of the pandemic'.[52,53] Therefore, if Big Tech had not taken direct advantage of the emergency, the crisis reinforced the long-term strategy to own, *de facto*, critical parts of the public sector, not to mention foreign control of the whole hardware and telecommunication infrastructure.

We sought help from Big Tech. We believed they could rid us of the virus. But they have forced us into a walled garden or a golden cage. Having denounced Big Tech's invasion of our privacy and their accumulation of every kind of information about us, the authorities have had to acknowledge their dependence upon them. During the peak of the pandemic, the world survived working thanks to the Internet and information technology. But what if tomorrow Apple, Google, or Microsoft decided to revoke all licences to use their computer programmes obliging us to acquire a 'brand new' operating system? Or what if they changed the terms of use of their cloud services? Nothing could prevent them from taking these actions as a business strategy or as a result of a presidential executive order, like the one that forced Google to divorce Huawei or caused Venezuela to be abruptly banned from accessing subscription, cloud-based services provided by the software giant Adobe.[54]

As mentioned, culture has been a conspicuous factor in the contest against the pandemic. We have seen how China, South Korea, and Taiwan deployed a vast, powerful, and well-designed information management infrastructure that existed prior to Coronavirus, not because of it. Little, if any, of this infrastructure was 'open source' or 'free software', nonetheless there was *public*, trusted control exercised over them. This demonstrates that it is not necessary to bar private technologies from the civil service, but

---

51 Angius & Zorloni 2020.
52 Soltero 2020.
53 Giles 2020.
54 On 7 October 2019, complying with US Presidential Executive Order n. 13884, (www.treasury.gov/resource-center/sanctions/Programs/Documents/13884.pdf) Adobe prevented its Venezuelan customers from accessing its subscription, cloud-based service, depriving them of the possibility to obtain updates, re-installs software, and access online content. The US Government recently revoked the ban on Adobe products and services, but the issue of who controls information technology is, in principle, unaffected.

The politics of the pandemic   131

rather asserting clear and firm public control that is required; this obviates becoming slave to the private sector. Retaining control over the public policing of digital information also helps to create mutual trust between citizen and State that may reduce or even eliminate the atavistic fear of technology. This is crucial since, as we discussed in Chapter 3, only social exposure to technology can generate the cultural antibodies to repel the virus of fear in the body of fundamental rights. But this can only be achieved if the State does not assert its control over the building of an information-based society, and ensures that its rule is apparent to citizens with the possibility for them to operate as civil watchdogs.

We must terminate the mutual distrust between citizen and state. It is this cultural lockdown that inhibits the successful benefits of information technology. It is, however, worth asking whether the alarmist debate about the role of technology has been negatively affected by a specific and limited intellectual position fuelled by an *a priori* repudiation of technology born in apocalyptic circles. Among many intellectuals there has been a regrettably Luddite outlook toward science and technology. This is particularly apparent in the discussion regarding the power and duty of the State to guarantee public order and security through the use of technology.

Until the outbreak of the pandemic, this debate was mostly based on virtual hypotheses and 'binary' oppositions between public power and fundamental rights without a test bench capable of providing experimental evidence. The abstract nature of the discourse oscillated between the dystopian and the enthusiastic adherence to the idea of a continuous, irresistible, and 'positive-by-definition' technological progress. This has created considerable inertia in respect of the design of a coordinated notion of technological public policy. As a result, the debate is trapped in the dualism of 'freedom and safety' or in one that contrasts 'privacy' with 'global control' and which views China as the only interlocutor, beyond which there lurk the proverbial lions.

The higher the level of mutual trust, the more extensive is the natural intertwining of information technology into daily life and the interaction with the public sector. It is no coincidence that Northern European countries such as Sweden,[55] Norway,[56] Finland,[57] and Iceland[58] (where the trust

55 European Union Commission. 2019. Digital Government Factsheet 2019, Sweden. https ://joinup.ec.europa.eu/sites/default/files/inline-files/Digital_Government_Factsheets_Swed en_2019.pdf (Visited 17 July 2020).
56 European Union Commission. 2019. Digital Government Factsheet 2019, Norway. https ://joinup.ec.europa.eu/sites/default/files/inline-files/Digital_Government_Factsheets_Norw ay_2019.pdf (Visited 17 July 2020).
57 European Union Commission. 2019. Digital Government Factsheet 2019, Finland. https ://joinup.ec.europa.eu/sites/default/files/inline-files/Digital_Government_Factsheets_Finl and_2019.pdf (Visited 17 July 2020).
58 European Union Commission. 2019. Digital Government Factsheet 2019, Finland. https ://joinup.ec.europa.eu/sites/default/files/inline-files/Digital_Government_Factsheets_Icel and_2019.pdf (Visited 18 June 2020).

132   The politics of the pandemic

index is very high, fundamental rights are strongly protected and are an essential part of public policy) score equally high marks in the ranking of digital government. And trust has been the keyword for the success of those Far Eastern societies that many years ago substantially incorporated information technology into the operations of their civil service. Far from being new bastions of democracy, South Korea and Taiwan have managed to establish a larger space for reflection on the role of science and technology in the public sector.

These examples demonstrate that techno-control is an extremely practical instrument in the centralized management of security and states of emergency. But they also reveal that extended and invasive public technological control do not automatically translate into irreversible limitations of individual rights such privacy and free speech. Compared with the asphyxiated European debate, this is a breath of fresh air: government choices have been the subject of public debate, communicated effectively, and implemented without spawning alarm for the survival of democracy. This balances the need to do 'whatever it takes' to manage an emergency while respecting a principle of gradualness in the (albeit generally inevitable) limitation of fundamental freedoms.

There are, however, three limits to such a choice. The first is purely political: it is necessary to accelerate technological modernization of society on the basis of clear choices (digitalization, interoperability, interconnection). National or supranational (EU) sovereignty over hardware infrastructures (telecom networks, computers, and peripherals) is unrealistic. A software Independence Day may be on the horizon. National sovereignty over digital identity and data already exists. By stating that the EU does not relinquish its duty to protect citizens' data including when they are processed abroad,[59] the European Court of Justice reinforced the prospect of ending the growing role of the private sector as online identity-keeper. It is meaningless that my social network account is not a substitute for a (digitally issued) State ID, if through the very same account I can access online services, pay remotely, and so on. De facto, one of the various Big Tech corporations can enforce a power that belongs to the State. It is up to the data protection authorities of member States to demonstrate that they are capable to perform this role: *hic Rhodus, hic salta*.

But data sovereignty is not only about privacy and free speech. As we emphasized in Chapter 4, the pandemic highlights the fundamental importance of public control over data or, rather, whether or not there is a limit to this control: private companies working for governments might use citizens' data to train their machine-learning algorithm and improve their systems

---

59 Court of Justice of the European Union. Press Release No 91/20—The Court of Justice invalidates Decision 2016/1250 on the adequacy of the protection provided by the EU–US Data Protection Shield, 16 July 2020. Luxembourg.

The politics of the pandemic   133

rendering them more powerful than those available to a State—and reap the financial rewards.

It is essential to consider the acceptability of a condition under which access to fundamental data such as those essential for contact tracing and medical research (but also for law enforcement) are left to the goodwill of private multinationals that unilaterally decide—occasionally shielding behind their duty to 'protect fundamental rights'—whether, to whom, how, and above all, when these data should be made available. Moreover, it needs to be asked whether it is a sustainable model, at least from the point of view of state sovereignty, that the civil service should use file formats, software applications, and hardware withdrawn from public control. A clear decision is urgently required because as the pandemic has demonstrated those who control data, control information and, ultimately, power. Hence, the key question is whether we can continue to permit public control over digital identity and data.

Centralizing the management of digital identity certainly has the merit of preventing foreign entities from accumulating information of any kind on citizens and protects fundamental rights such as free speech and privacy. On the other hand, as the Chinese experience shows, employing platforms as an access point to utilize otherwise unusable services becomes a tool of censorship, punitive fines, and social ostracism. In fact, there are documented cases of the arrest of dissidents who reported unwelcome events,[60] and with threats of deletion of accounts on social networks without which, given the high degree of digitization of services of any kind, normal social or business activities are effectively thwarted.[61] Again, the risk here is to retreat into the false dichotomy that precludes a fundamental digital transformation.

To escape this risk the second factor of social nature is pertinent. Without social acceptance of these systems, gradually introduced and managed democratically and transparently, it will be difficult to achieve an adequate degree of social acceptability of an advanced technological infrastructure. Nowadays no one complains about ATMs, automated motorway access, online flight and travel reservations, or other similar digital services. They have not, in general, created a dystopian, panopticon society. But social acceptability of new technology, especially if it is in the hands of a State, is a more complex phenomenon:

> Technology is a social practice that embodies the capacity of societies to transform themselves by creating and manipulating not only physical objects, but also symbols and cultural forms. It is an illusion that scientific and socioeconomic drivers are the sole elements determining the destiny of a technology. Although they are important, what is really

60 Le Belzic 2020.
61 Op. cit.

134   *The politics of the pandemic*

crucial is the way in which a human community 'metabolizes' a new technology, that is the way in which a new technology becomes part of the mental landscape of people living in that society.[62]

Attitudes toward new technology are based less on actual understanding or expertise than perception. 'Thirty-one potential determinants which emerged from the coding scheme were found to influence public acceptance of new technologies ... Of these, perceived risk was found to be the most frequently investigated determinant'.[63] Equally, if perception is the key, it is no surprise that psychometrics are back in fashion when designing public policy.[64] But, and this is critical, the temptation to lure individuals into acceptance by unscrupulous consent manipulation techniques such as nudging is very powerful. Nudging and other internal propaganda tools are precisely what prevents (or breaches) the formation of a fair rapport. Be it State-run shepherding or an attempt by the executive to bypass parliamentary control by pursuing its own agenda rather than by transparent public policy, these techniques inhibit a trusted pact from being sealed.

As a consequence there is the final factor. Until an accord of transparency between State and citizen is (re)built and honoured, the primeval and mutual distrust of political power will obstruct progress toward this end. Among the many contradictions exposed at every level by COVID-19 is the realization that, even if we desired one, a Taiwanese or South Korean technological solution would have been impossible in the UK, Italy, or most Western countries. This is not, as suggested above, because of cultural, political, or legal differences between the Far East and the West but—trivially—because of the different approaches to the integration of information technology in the public sector that too often compels the use of brawn rather than brain.

Yet again, if the answers have to come from the abstract contrast between ideological positions and slogans, they are unlikely to produce a rational outcome. On the contrary, if a lesson can be drawn from South Korean and Taiwanese experiences, it is that instead of paralyzing the activity of decision-makers with apodictic and aprioristic statements, the dichotomy of surveillance vs freedom can be overcome by transparency that allows an effective control on the use of information technology by public authorities. The point, therefore, is not to assert the public or private nature of information, but to establish the principle that data and information should be managed in such a way that, should the need arise, they could be immediately placed into the system. Caution is, however, required:

62   Mordini 2007.
63   Gupta, Fischer, & Frewe 2012.
64   Fischhoff et al. 1978.

Government and policymakers want to engage the public in a dialogue about the conduct and consequences of science and increasingly seek to actively involve citizens in decision-making processes. Implicit in this thinking is that greater transparency and public inclusion will help dispel fears associated with new scientific advancements, foster greater public trust in those accountable, and ultimately increase the acceptability of new technologies. Less understood, however, are public perceptions about such high-level involvement in science and how these map onto public trust and attitudes within a diverse population. ... Our findings run contrary to assumptions that public involvement in science will foster greater trust and lead to a climate of greater acceptance for genetic technology ... Whereas trust is positively correlated with more permissive attitudes about technologies such as cloning and gene therapy, people who believe in high-level public involvement are less likely to think that these technologies should be allowed than those who do not.[65]

But how is such trust built? As astonishing as it may seem, the answer is already there: protect the rule of law and fundamental rights:

A democratic government will not survive long if it does not build and sustain the trust of its citizens. Trust is a must in government, and not only for democratic government. Ironically, even rulers who may have come to power through a coup d'état or another form of unconstitutional seizure of power can gradually build trust among citizens, respect their rights, and enjoy popular support. In contrast, rulers elected through fair and free elections may rapidly lose trust if they do not deliver and live up to people's expectations. Trust in government is the central element of good governance—it can be built up with sound policies enhancing people's welfare and safety. But it can also be lost. It is not something a priori given.[66]

If citizens believe that the government plays by the book and does not seek shortcuts when balancing the public interest with individual rights, it will usually satisfy the test of accountability. People will be more willing to live in a technology- and data-driven society. Trust in politics and politicians is at a low ebb, and it is not easy to establish or rebuild. While there is truth in Verga's aphorism '*al giorno d'oggi per conoscere un uomo bisogna mangiare sette salme di sale*'[67] *sette salme* may not be enough when it comes to trusting politicians.

---

65 Barnett, Cooper, & Senior 2007. See too Kohn 2008.
66 Popovski 2010: 234.
67 Verga 1881. 'To know a man you need to eat more than a ton of salt together'.

136 *The politics of the pandemic*

References

Angius, Raffaele and Luca Zorloni. 2020. '30mila caselle email della scuola italiana passano a Microsoft', *Wired.it*, 6 July. www.wired.it/internet/web/2020/07/06/microsoft-scuola/ (Visited 17 July 2020).

Aurelius, Marcus. 1943. *Tὰ εἰς ἑαυτόν VI, 26. Translated by Andrea Monti from the Italian Edition I Ricordi*. Torino: Einaudi.

Barnett, Julie, Cooper H. and Vitoria Senior. 2007. 'Belief in Public Efficacy, Trust, and Attitudes Toward Modern Genetic Science', *Risk Analysis* 27(4): 921–933. doi:10.1111/j.1539-6924.2007.00932.x (Visited 17 July 2020).

Bingham, Tom. 2010. *The Rule of Law*. Harmondsworth: Penguin.

Breen, Michael. 2020. 'What's Fueling Korea's Coronavirus Success—And Relapse', *Politico*, 15 May. www.politico.eu/article/whats-fueling-south-korea-coronaviru s-covid19-success-and-relapse/ (Visited 14 July 2020).

Bruun, Christer. 2012. 'La mancanza di prove di un effetto catastrofico della "peste antonina" (dal 166 DC in poi)', in Lo Cascio, Elio (ed.). *L'impatto della'peste antonina'*. Bari: Edipuglia.

Castellucci, Ignazio. 2012. 'Rule of Law and Legal Complexity in the People's Republic of China', *Quaderni del Dipartimento di Scienze Giuridiche* 103: 5.

Cockburn, Frederick. 1867. *Charge of the Lord Chief Justice of England to the Grand Jury at the Central Criminal Court in the Case of the Queen Against Nelson & Brand*, 2nd ed. London: William Ridgway.

Craig, Paul. 1997. 'Formal and Substantive Conceptions of the Rule of Law: An Analytical Framework', *Public Law* 467.

Dicey, A.V. 1885. *Introduction to the Study of the Law of the Constitution, Classic Reprint*. London: Forgotten Books, 2012.

Donadoni, Eugenio. 1963–1966. *Dizionario letterario Bompiani delle opere e dei personaggi*. Milano: Bompiani.

Duncan-Jones, Richard. 2018. 'The Antonine Plague Revisited', Arctos. *Acta Philologica Fennica* 52: 44–45.

Dworkin, Ronald. 1986. *Law's Empire*. Cambridge: Harvard University Press.

Fischhoff, Baruch, Paul Slovic, Sara Lichtenstein, Stephen Read and Barbara Combs. 1978.'How Safe is Safe Enough? A Psychometric Study of Attitudes Towards Technological Risks and Benefits', *Policy Sciences* 9(2): 127–152.

Foscolo, Ugo. 1867. *Opere Complete di Ugo Foscolo*, Vol. I. Naples. Francesco Lubrano.

Fraenkel, Ernst. 1941–2017. *The Dual State*. New York: Oxford University Press.

Friedman, Steven. 2020. 'COVID-19 has Blown Away the Myth About "First" and "Third" World Competence', *The Conversation*, 13 May. https://theconv ersation.com/covid-19-has-blown-away-the-myth-about-first-and-third-world-c ompetence-138464 (Visited 13 July 2020).

Frischmann, Brett. 2020. 'Is Smart Technology Making Us Dumb?', *Scientific American*, 27 December. https://blogs.scientificamerican.com/observations/is-sm art-technology-making-us-dumb/ (Visited 4 July 2020).

Fuller, Lon L. 1969. *The Morality of Law*, rev edn. New Haven, CN and London: Yale University Press.

Gardner, Daniel K. 2014. *Confucianism. A Very Short Introduction*. Oxford: Oxford University Press.

Giles, Martin. 2020. 'Free Software That Businesses, Schools and Others Can Use During the COVID-19 Crisis', *Forbes*, online edition, 4 June www.forbes.com/

sites/martingiles/2020/03/19/free-software-for-businesses-and-schools-covid19/?ss=cio-network#2e02079d752d (Visited 17 July 2020).

Grant, James A. 2017. 'The Ideals of the Rule of Law', Oxford Journal of Legal Studies 37: 383.

Gupta, Nidhi, Arnout Fischer and Lynn Frewer. 2012. 'Socio-Psychological Determinants of Public Acceptance of Technologies: A Review', *Public Understanding of Science* 21(7): 782–795. https://doi.org/10.1177/0963662510392485 (Visited 17 July 2020).

Harper, Kyle. 2019. *The Fate of Rome*, The Princeton History of the Ancient World. Princeton: Princeton University Press.

Ioannidis, John. 2020. 'Coronavirus Disease 2019: The Harms of Exaggerated Information and Non-Evidence-Based Measures', *European Journal of Clinical Investigation* 50(2). https://doi.org/10.1111/eci.13222 (Visited 4 July 2020).

Kim, So Young. 2010. 'Do Asian Values Exist? Empirical Tests of the Four Dimensions of Asian Values', *Journal of East Asian Studies* 10: 315–344.

Kohn, Marek. 2008. *Trust: Self-Interest and the Common Good*. Oxford: Oxford University Press.

Le Belzic, Sébastien. 2020. 'Coronavirus in China', *DW Documentary*, 17 March, minute 18:10. https://youtu.be/3K3fy5eKeuM?t=1090 (Visited 17 July 2020).

Luciani, Massimo. 2020. 'Il sistema delle fonti del diritto alla prova dell'emergenza', Liber amicorum per Pasquale Costanzo. www.giurcost.org/LIBERAMICORUM/luciani_scrittiCostanzo.pdf (Visited 17 July 2020).

Manzoni, Alessandro. 1827. *I promessi sposi, English edition, The Betrothed*. London: Richard Bentley.

Martin, Timothy and Marcus Walker. 2020. 'East vs. West: Coronavirus Fight Tests Divergent Strategies', *The Wall Street Journal*, online edition, 13 May. www.wsj.com/articles/east-vs-west-coronavirus-fight-tests-divergent-strategies-11584110308 (Visited 13 July 2020).

Mattern, Susan. 2018. *The Prince of Medicine*. Oxford: Oxford University Press.

McBride-Folkers, Kelly and Arthur Caplan. 2020. 'False Hope about Coronavirus Treatments', *Scientific American*, 4 March. https://blogs.scientificamerican.com/observations/false-hope-about-coronavirus-treatments/ (Visited 4 July 2020).

Mir, Raoof. 'India's Media Must Promote Science, Not Superstition, in COVID-19 Fight', *Nikkei Asian Review*, 6 April. https://asia.nikkei.com/Opinion/India-s-media-must-promote-science-not-superstition-in-COVID-19-fight (Visited 4 July 2020).

Miyashita, Hiroshi. 2020. Covid-19 and Data Protection in Japan. Blogdroiteuropéen. https://blogdroiteuropeen.com/2020/07/31/covid-19-and-data-protection-in-japan-by-hiroshi-miyashita/ (Visited 27 July 2020).

Monti, Andrea. 2020. 'Le questioni irrisolte dello stato di emergenza', Formiche.net, 14 July. https://formiche.net/2020/07/stato-emergenza-covid-19/ (Visited 15 July 2020).

Monti, Andrea and Raymond Wacks. 2019. *Protecting Personal Information: The Right to Privacy Reconsidered*. Oxford: Hart Publishing.

Mordini, Emilio. 2007. 'Technology and Fear: Is Wonder the Key?', *Trends in Biotechnology* 25(12). https://doi.org/10.1016/j.tibtech.2007.08.012 (Visited 17 July 2020).

Park, Nathan. 2020. 'Confucianism Isn't Helping Beat the Coronavirus', *Foreign Policy*, 2 April. https://foreignpolicy.com/2020/04/02/confucianism-south-korea-coronavirus-testing-cultural-trope-orientalism/ (Visited 13 July 2020).

138 *The politics of the pandemic*

Popovski, Vesselin. 2010. 'Conclusion: Trust is a Must in Government', in Cheema, Shabbir and Popovski, Vesselin (eds.). *Building Trust in Government: Innovations in Governance Reform in Asia*. New York: United Nations University Press.

Raz, Joseph. 1977. 'The Rule of Law and its Virtue', *Law Quarterly Review* 93: 195.

Raz, Joseph. 2019. 'The Law's Own Virtue', *Oxford Journal of Legal Studies* 39: 1.

Robertson, Donald. 2020. 'Stoicism in the Time of Plague'. https://medium.com/stoicism-philosophy-as-a-way-of-life/stoicism-in-the-time-of-plague-652759c274b2 (Visited 1 July 2020).

Sabbatani, Sergio and Sirio Fiorino. 2009. 'La peste antonina e il declino dell'Impero Romano. Ruolo della guerra partica e della guerra marcomannica tra il 164 e il 182 d.C. nella diffusione del contagio', in InfezMed. *Le Infezioni in Medicina*. Salerno: University of Salerno, n. 4 261–275.

Soltero, Javier. 2020. 'Helping Businesses and Schools Stay Connected in Response to Coronavirus'. 3 March. https://cloud.google.com/blog/products/g-suite/helping-businesses-and-schools-stay-connected-in-response-to-coronavirus (Visited 17 July 2020).

Stiglitz, Joseph, Jean-Paul Fitoussi and Martine Durand (eds.) 2018. *For Good Measure: Advancing Research on Well-being Metrics Beyond GDP*. Paris: OECD Publishing. https://doi.org/10.1787/9789264307278-en. https://read.oecd-ilibrary.org/economics/for-good-measure/average-trust-in-others-across-109-countries-2014_9789264307278-graph32-en#page1 (Visited 14 July 2020).

Thompson, Derek. 2020. 'What's Behind South Korea's COVID-19 Exceptionalism?', *The Atlantic*. online edition. www.theatlantic.com/ideas/archive/2020/05/whats-south-koreas-secret/611215/ (Visited 14 July 2020).

Verga, Giovanni. 1881. I Malavoglia. Milan Fratelli Treves editori. English edition, Craig, Mary (trans.). 1890. The House of Medlar-Tree. Continental Classics.

Wingfield-Hayes, Rupert. 'Coronavirus: Japan's Mysteriously Low Virus Death Rate', *BBC News*, 4 July. www.bbc.com/news/world-asia-53188847 (Visited 15 July 2020).

Zouev, Alexandre. 2020. 'COVID and the Rule of Law: A Dangerous Balancing Act'. www.un.org/en/coronavirus/covid-and-rule-law-dangerous-balancing-act (Visited 4 July 2020).

Epilogue

Lockdown, social distancing, testing and tracing, face covering: the world has acquired a new vernacular and a transformed social order. The pandemic has not only ended a million lives, it has profoundly changed significant features of our existence. We find it hard to accept the impossibility of a risk-free world, but the reality of disease is anything but novel in developing countries.

The impact of COVID-19 on public policy continues to evolve. It will require decades before a final assessment of the efficacy of our response can be made. Among the most pertinent phenomena, once the initial global fear has subsided, is the appearance in the public arena of the politicization of the pandemic. The unrealistic hope of a policy that can guarantee a Coronavirus-free society affects the choices open to a government. The social fatigue caused by fear for the future is being driven by extremist political movements which are gaining momentum even in democratic countries such as Germany and Britain.

The economy, employment, technology, the media, and the provision of medical services are only the most conspicuous elements that COVID-19 has shaken. Yet, while nations may have shared semantics, divergent strategies have contributed to an improbable rise of nationalism, most notably in the pursuit of vaccination against the virus. Competition between research institutes in various countries has led the World Health Organization to sound an early warning against vaccine nationalism. It has warned against the withholding or theft of data and other key resources as occurred with medical supplies in the early phases of the contagion.

Nevertheless, despite the reality that a vaccine may be many months away, it has been 'weaponized' in the diplomatic arena. Obtaining a vaccine offers the prospect of creating international alliances or, out of necessity, forging new ones thereby shaking the already fragile global balance of power. The United States asserts that a Chinese vaccine may be deployed against the West, a claim fervently denied by Beijing. It is rumoured that India is collaborating with Russia to produce batches of the *Sputnik V* vaccine, while trying to secure priority delivery from all the international manufacturers.

140 *Epilogue*

The understandably desperate quest for a dependable diagnosis, effective therapy, or cure has spawned an irrational search for a scientific 'break-through'. The apparent haste with which Russia patented the first vaccine has raised concerns about its safety owing to the alleged lack of comprehensive trials. Moreover, unreasonable expectations have been stoked by the media which continues to broadcast reports of the early results of research—still in pre-print stage—which await peer review. Whether this is sensationalism, commercialism, or ineptitude, it has also been instrumental in stimulating anti-Chinese sentiment, as some of the studies (one rejected several times, another not yet reviewed) have been exploited to strengthen the contention that China is responsible for originating and spreading the virus.

The fear is frequently expressed that, having adopted Draconian measures to stem the disease, governments are unlikely to revoke them after the pandemic has been subjugated. The eventual acquiescence by the public to extensive surveillance, for example, may, it is suggested, encourage its adoption as a permanent feature of political or crime control. No less disquieting are some of the developments on the international stage. Anxieties about domestic disorder generated by the strict regulation of safety measures have been seized upon as a justification for the purchase of arms and other contrivances of crowd control. Some countries have expressed unease about the possibility of neighbouring nations exploiting their perceived COVID-induced weakness.

The threat to democracy is also evident among those repressive countries whose traditions of authoritarianism, corruption, and bureaucracy have combined to thwart the management of the pandemic. Brazil and other Latin American countries are the most palpable illustrations.

On the economic front, different EU political blocs have had to wrestle with various means by which to achieve economic recovery. This has exposed disagreeable prejudice against certain member States (especially Italy) which have resisted any checks on expenditure of funds provided to assist renewal.

The significant differences in the individual responses to the challenges posed by the pandemic demonstrate the role of country-specific cultures and approaches. The Swedish and Japanese approaches rely on trust in collective responsibility rather than stringent lockdown provisions compelling the wearing of masks and adopting approved social behaviour. To adjudge such measures as failures on the basis of their death toll is both specious and tendentious. Statistics, as we argue in Chapter 2, have been greatly abused and misused by governments and the media; they are a precarious basis for comparison. But it is clear that this form of collective-responsibility policing would have little success in countries with a more individualistic ethos.

Broadly speaking, those nations which fared best in the initial struggle to contain the disease continue to deliver positive results, and vice versa. In other words, domestic political conflict and economic ruptures prevented

Epilogue 141

less advanced countries from overcoming or at least curtailing the spread of the virus.

The pandemic has revealed a number of weaknesses in the structure and operation of the civil services of most nations. It has also exposed the vulnerability of the economic order; the frantic compulsion to avoid collapse has occluded the elimination of the impediments to greater efficiency. And it has engendered a propensity to blame COVID-19 for all the ills we are currently enduring. This is plainly an overstatement. There are deeper elements of the world order that lie at the heart of our discord and distress.

The advent of the second wave of the virus ought to give us pause to consider whether, in our pursuit of materialism and consumerism, we may have lost sight of some of the more enduring and essential values of democratic freedom and the rule of law.

15 October 2020

Index

Note: Locators followed by 'n' refer to notes.

5G technology 117
9/11 terrorist outrage 2
1860 India's Penal Code 55
1905 October Revolution 84
1936 British Public Order Act 83
1948 Gallup failure 87–88

Adleman, Leonard 90
advertising 18–19, 22n26, 51, 58, 88, 96–97
Agonism 51
AIDS 9, 91
Alexander of Abonoteichus 113
Amazon Web Services 102
American Big Tech firms 57
Annan, Kofi 27
anti-Chinese sentiment 140
antiscientific public policy approach 2
Antonine Plague of 165 AD 6
anxiety 27, 42, 51, 123
aphorism 135
applied psychology research 88
artificial intelligence 2, 60, 115
Aurelius, Marcus 114
authoritarianism 73, 140
Autonomous Logistics Information System (ALIS) 23

Badoglio, Pietro 25
Behavioural economics 31
bellum omnium contra omnes 3
Benedict, Ruth 29
Bernays, Edward 20, 22, 85, 95, 96
Bluetooth, use of 65
bombing of Hiroshima and Nagasaki 25
border protection 69
British Locomotive Act of 1865 63

card-based filing system 84
China: Confucian' acquiescence 2, 70; contact tracing in 61; criteria-set to define COVID-19 39; delaying existence of Coronavirus 8; Health Code system 61; infrastructure 61–63, 120, 130; political abuse of psychiatry 54; social scoring 85; *vs.* United States, Cold War 50, 120; vaccine 139; WeChat (the messaging system) 62
Chomsky, Noam 20
The Chrysanthemum and the Sword 29
Churchill, Winston 26
Civic Assistants 74–75
'Civic Guard' 74–75
civil coexistence 122
civil liberties/rights: compulsory medical screening 54; disease control authorities 48; government attitude 1–2; herd immunity 53; *ignes fatui* 51; mass surveillance programmes 49; media organization *openDemocracy* 102; media's attitude 52; perception of restricted rights 50–54; political control by ruling parties 53; public policy and security 53; security and freedom 48; self-preservation 50; stockpiling in supermarkets 51
Cold War II 50, 120
collective responsibility 140
co-morbidities in death 40
computer-based trait predictions 98
computer revolution in surveillance and control: 1990s, Internet-connected resources 89; algorithm 'RSA' 90; FTP server 90; hacking

Index 143

movement 89; Ninth Circuit 90–91, 90n31; Pretty Good Privacy or PGP 90–91; pro-privacy and anti-techno-surveillance culture 89
Confucianism 2, 17, 70, 126
contact tracing computer programmes 61, 64–65
Contagious Disease Prevention and Control Act (CDPCA) 62
courts: and abuses of power 74; 'Asian values' and Confucianism 126; China's 'rule by law' 125; culture 127; freedom of expression 124; impact of market economy 125; 'stay-at-home' recommendation 126; two-stage *coup*, Nazi party 123; values and the law 123
COVID-19: death 41; COVID-19 Tools Accelerator 8; definition 39; fine-based policing 75; marshals 74; probable case 39–40; probable death 40–41; spread of 112–113
credit scoring surveillance 86
Crystallizing Public Opinion 96
Curtis, Adam 88
cybercrime 49

data-gathering policing 93
data-led approach 102, 103
data scientists 81
data sovereignty 132
data theft 99–101
data transparency and reproducibility 29
decision-making process 28, 37, 135
dehumanization 27
democracy, threat to 140
democratic governance 122n25
depression 50, 51
Dharma, concept of 17
Diceyan concept of rule of law 121–122
dichotomy 10, 133–134
Dichter, Ernest 86
Diffie, Whitfield 90
digital contact tracing 2
digital hygiene policies 92
digital identity 132–133
digital technology 12
Disclosure and Barring Service Check 59
disease control authorities 48
DNA police databases 60
Draconian quarantine measures 9, 42, 120

The Dual State 122
'duty of salvation' 37n64
Dworkin, Ronald 55

ecological security 4
e-commerce revolution 86
Edsel project, shipwreck 87
emotional distress 51
enforcement of legal provisions 68
EU General Data Protection Regulation (GDPR) 66
exposure notification 82; app' 64; location tracking to 66; software 64, 66

face covering 139
face-to-face manipulative techniques 97
fact-based surveillance 94
fact-checking organizations 58
Fauci, Anthony 11
fingerprint filing-system 83
Five Factor Model (FFM) 97–98
five-pillar strategy, United Kingdom 37
Fraenkel, Ernst 73, 122–123
'free-as-in-free-beer' strategy 130
freedom of expression 12, 124
free speech and fake news prevention: 1860 India's Penal Code 55; British reaction to Coronavirus fake news 57; curbing of free speech 54; fact-checking organizations 58; Hungarian anti-Coronavirus fake news legislation 54; Irish Criminal Justice Public Order Act 55; Italian Penal Code 55; Japanese Broadcasting Act 55; problem of (lack of) culture and education 58
French Indochina war 28
French *la Terreur* 17
French Revolution 18
Freud 96
FTP server 90
fundamental rights and governments: authoritarianism 73; border protection 69; Civic Assistants 74–75; 'Civic Guard' 74–75; Confucian acquiescence 70; courts and abuses of power 74; COVID-19 fine-based policing 75; COVID marshals 74; national culture 69; public outrage 75; public security database 69; stay-at-home orders 70; stringent regulatory controls 69–70; use of information and telecommunication 76

144 *Index*

geo-fencing-based quarantine 66
geolocation 66, 82
geopolitics: China's delaying the existence of Coronavirus 8; Iran's refusal to US assistance 8; monitoring disease 9
Germany: comprehensive testing programme 38; Nazi Germany 73n70; protection of rights 2; psycho-sociological experiments 15
global war on terrorism 49
Guardie Civiche case 75
Gulf and Iraqi wars 28–29

hacking movement 89
Health Code system 61
Hellman, Martin E 90
herd immunity 53
The Hidden Persuaders 96
History of Dharmasastra 17
Hitler 123
Hobbes, Thomas 3, 51
homo economicus 30–31
Hong Kong, close of border with Mainland China 7
Huanan market 3
human behaviour: psychology of 95; understanding 95
Hungarian anti-Coronavirus fake news legislation 54

ignes fatui 51
Illiberal democracies 13
Imperial Roman Variola plague 6
Independentism 6
Indian caste system 18
individual liberty, limitations 9–10, 74
information and telecommunication 76
information technology: case study *see* technologies of information (case study); data-gathering policing, need for 93; deficiencies of the Internet Protocol version IV (Ipv4) 91; digital hygiene policies 92; fact-based surveillance 94; information about the AIDS virus 91; predictive technologies and automated 'AI-powered' analysis 94; surveillance capitalism 92, 92n33
Insurrection Act of 1807 75
Internet-based, data driven economy 30
Internet DNS queries 59
Internet Protocol version IV (Ipv4) 91
Iran, refusal to US assistance 8

Irish Criminal Justice Public Order Act 55
Italian Medicine Agency 36
Italian Penal Code 55
Italy: attitudes toward technology 133–134; communication with the public 128; culture 130; data sovereignty 132; distrust between citizen and state 131; 'free-as-in-free-beer' strategy 130; management of digital identity 133; National Civil Protection 38; 'positive-by-definition' technological progress 131; public health system's efficiency 10; public security and health emergencies 129; regional ordinances 7; regulations 1–2; techno-control 132; technology policing 129; transparency and public inclusion 135; trust 135

Japan: anti-influenza drug 36; Japanese Broadcasting Act 5, 55; low virus death rate 126; public policy 68–69; respect toward central authority 2; scholars 68

Korea Centers for Disease Control and Prevention (KCDC) 62
Korean war 28
Kurokawa, Mariko 68

Le Bon, Gustave 96
legal system 63, 69, 72, 73, 120, 122, 125
liberalism 17
Liu, Eric 16
local vaccination activity 60
lockdown 1, 6–7, 11, 25, 67, 70, 73–74, 76, 129, 131, 139–140

Machiavelli, Niccolò 19
Machtpolitik 25
Magna Carta 18
malevolence 67
Manzoni, Alessandro 120
market economy, impact of 125
Marxism 17
masks, protective 82, 92, 126, 140
mass persuasion 10
mass surveillance programmes 49, 59; card-based filing system 84; data from the Census Bureau 84; fingerprint filing-system 83; Police fingerprint archives 83; 'the Third Section (Tsarist political police) 84
mass swab-testing 37–38

Index 145

Mayu, Arimoto 68
Médecins Sans Frontières 7n20
media: 5G technology 117; attitude
52; electronic media 116–120;
misinformation and fake news
117–118; negative impact on
policymakers 118–119; socialized 5
medicine: practice based on science 33;
socialized 5
'Me Generation,' emergence of 96
MERS 2, 8, 62, 64
Microsoft 102, 107, 130
*Milizia volontaria per la sicurezza
nazionale* 75
Ministry of Health and Welfare
(MOHW) 62

nationalism: blocking delivery of
masks 7; increased autonomy 7;
and independentism 6; vaccine
nationalism 8
neo-Confucianism 125
neuro-linguistic programming (NLP)
21, 97
neurosciences 30, 95
Newton, Isaac 31
NHS-owned algorithm 105
Night of the Living Dead 3
Nineteen Eighty-Four 19, 57
Ninth Circuit 90–91, 90n31
non-deterministic dynamic
programming 30
North Africa and Middle East
geopolitical crises 2
nuclear *vs.* alternative energies 36

Obama, Barack 9, 96, 99
openDemocracy 102
Orwell, George 19–20

Packard, Vance 96
personality-traits profiling 101
plague, effects 6, 43, 48, 67, 114–115, 120
police(ing): checks 42; DNA police
databases 60; fingerprint archives 83;
powers to 71–72; scrutiny in public
52; technology 129
policy and persuasion: business
relationships 23; consent
management 19; convincing people
22; direct and invasive controls 20;
neuro-linguistic programming (NLP)
21; 'nudge theory 21; political goal-
setting 24; PsyOps 19

post-traumatic stress disorder 51
power: 'AI-powered' analysis 94;
courts and abuses of 74; 'duty of
salvation' 37n64; executive, role
of 11; five-pillar strategy, United
Kingdom 37; limitations 18; nuclear
vs. alternative energies 36; to police
71–72; of predictive technology 115;
role of 67–68; science and *see* science
and power; science as instrument of
regulation 37; to social networking
and search engine 11–12; sources of
civic 16
praeteritio 26
pragmatism 27, 32
precautionary-principles 119–120
predictive' technologies and automated
'AI-powered' analysis 94
Pretty Good Privacy (PGP) 90–91
privacy and public safety: Bluetooth,
use of 65; Chinese, South Korean
infrastructure 61–63; with data
protection 61; DNA police databases
60; enforcement of legal provisions
68; exposure notification software
64; geo-fencing-based quarantine
66; Internet DNS queries 59;
Japanese public policy 68–69; local
vaccination activity 60; mass data-
gathering and surveillance 59; power,
role of 67–68; privacy 65; and public
safety 59–69; right of privacy with
data protection 61; rigorous contact
tracing 61; Taiwanese infrastructures
62–63; 'traditional' contact tracing
61; virus containment/eradication
programme 60
private profiling: applied psychology
research 88; bias by design
85; Chinese social scoring 85;
credit scoring surveillance 86;
psychoanalysis 87; public order
management 86
profiling 100; analytics tools 96;
computer-based trait predictions 98;
face-to-face manipulative techniques
97; Five Factor Model (FFM) 97–98;
neuro-linguistic programming 97;
neurosciences 95; psychology of
human behaviour 95; psychometrics
96–97; social networking 97;
technology of 95–99; understanding
human behaviour 95; *see also* private
profiling

146 *Index*

Propaganda 96
pro-privacy and anti-techno-surveillance culture 89
psychoanalysis 86–87, 96
psychology of the masses [Le Bon's] 96
psychometrics 19, 96–97
PsyOps 19
public administration 17, 35
public education 10, 59
public order management 86
public outrage 75
public policy: customs and ideas 17; definition 16; fundamental rights 18; power, limitations 18; and science 28; and security 53; sources of civic power 16
public relations 19
public security database 69
Putin, Vladimir 24
Python programming language 81

quarantine measures: Draconian 9, 42, 120; geo-fencing-based quarantine 66; homely application 43; stringent quarantine in authoritarian societies 10; *see also* lockdown

Reagan era, US perception management programme 53n17
Realpolitik 27, 85
Reeves, Rosser 97
Reich, Wilhelm 96
religious group-worshipping practices 63
restriction of rights: combating virus, Far Eastern countries 12–13; devastation, industrial and commercial 11; digital technology 12; lack of transparency in public policy 10; limitations on liberty 9–10; maintaining public's trust 9; mass persuasion and public education 10; power to social networking and search engine 11–12; relationship between law, rights, and economics 11; rich and poor disparities 11; role of executive power 11; stringent quarantine in authoritarian societies 10
Ricci, David 34
rigorous contact tracing 61
Rivest, Ronald 90
Romero, George 3
'RSA,' algorithm 90
Russia: 1905 October Revolution 84; 1917 Bolshevik *coup* in 17; adverse

consequences of the lockdown, oil price drop 7; Russian Federation 55n25; socialized healthcare systems 5; Stalinist 15

Sakharov, Andrei 34
SARS 2–4, 3, 4n5, 8
SARS-CoV-2 25
science and power: data transparency and reproducibility 29; decision-making process 28; dehumanization of the enemy 27; 'duty of salvation' 37n64; explanation *vs.* truth 30; five-pillar strategy, United Kingdom 37; giving advice and providing rough data 33; human life and economic stability 24; as instrument of regulation 37; Internet-based, data driven economy 30; medicine, practice based on science 33; neutrality *vs.* reality 33–35; non-deterministic dynamic programming 30; nuclear *vs.* alternative energies 36; policy and persuasion 19–24; political expediency 26; public administration 35; public policy 16–18; science and policy 33–34; scientific method 31–32; social science and security 28–30; statistics and social control *see* statistics
scientific method 16, 30–32
Second World War 15
self-preservation 50
service d'information du gouvernement ('SIG') 56
Shamir, Adi 90
Skype for Business 129
smallpox epidemic of 165, in Roman Empire 113–114
social and moral consequences 5
social distancing 11, 43, 61, 129, 139
social networking 12, 20, 21, 97, 116, 118, 124
social science and security 28–29, 30
South Korea: contact tracing strategy 61, 63; culture 127–128; massive testing of the population 40, 40n77; religious freedom and privacy 63; SARS in 2003 and MERS in 2015 2; social responsibility and governmental transparency 70
Spanish flu 4–6
Sputnik V vaccine 139

Index   147

statistics: calculating positive individuals 41; confirmed and probable cases 39–40; homely application of quarantine 43; media coverage 42; misperceptions, COVID evolution 41–42; social distancing 43
stay-at-home orders 70, 126
stockpiling in supermarkets 51
Storia della colonna infame 42
Sumption, Lord 72
superstition, science and: 'magic power' of predictive technology 115; misleading products and therapy 115–116
surveillance capitalism 92, 94, 97
surveillance obsession 101
surviving COVID 3–6; comparison with Spanish flu 5; disease control system in Taiwan 4; Huanan market 3; identification and spread 3; public policy and strategies 3; reassessment of legislative framework 6; social and moral consequences 5

Taiwan: disease control system 4; infrastructures 62–63; SARS and MERS 2; social responsibility and governmental transparency 70; technological and regulatory terms 62–63
Takahashi, Ikuo 68
Teams for universities and schools 129
technologies of information (case study): agreement 103; cognitive services 107; contract agreements 103–107; creation of data store 103; decision-making 108–109; five companies 102
technology policing 129
telescreen 19
Third Reich 124
The Tiananmen Papers 56

tracing: contact tracing computer programmes 61, 64–65; digital contact tracing 2; rigorous contact tracing 61; testing and 139; traditional contact 61
transparency and public inclusion 135
Truman, Harry S. 25
Trump, Donald 11, 116

United Kingdom: Coronavirus Act 2020 53; COVID marshals 74; impact of 'nudge theory' 21; National DNA database 35
United Nations, peacekeeping interventions 20
United States: atomic supremacy 15; *vs.* China, Cold War II 120; definition of 'COVID-19 case' 39; global surveillance 83; hacking movement 89; impact of 'nudge theory' 21

vaccine: Chinese 139; nationalism 8, 139; Russia patented 140; *Sputnik V* vaccine 139
values and law 123
Verga, Giovanni 135
Vietnam war 28
virus containment/eradication programme 60
von Clausewitz, Carl 26
von Hayek, Friedrich 31
Voodoo practitioners 15

wealth-based differences 2–3
WeChat (the messaging system) 62
western, educated, industrialized, rich, democratic (WEIRD) populations 98
wet markets 3
Wylie, Christopher 94

Yalta Big Three 25

Zimmermann, Philip 90–91

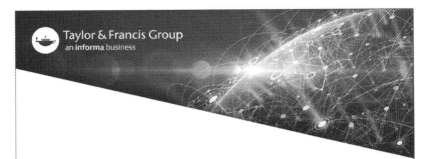

Printed in the United States
By Bookmasters